D1270868

In the Web of History
Gonzaga College and the Lincoln Assassination

In the Web of History
Gonzaga College and the
Lincoln Assassination

by Paul Warren

 '68

VELLUM An imprint of New Academia Publishing
Washington, DC

Copyright © 2008 by Paul Warren

VELLUM/New Academia Publishing, 2009

All rights reserved. No part of this book may be reproduced or transmitted in any form or by any means, electronic or mechanical, including photocopying, recording, or by any information storage and retrieval system.

Printed in the United States of America

ISBN 978-0-9818654-4-7

Contact author at pwarren@warren-news.com
Purchase book at GonzagaLincoln.com

New Academia Publishing, LLC
P.O. Box 27420
Washington, DC 20038-7420
www.newacademia.com - info@newacademia.com

To the Revs. Anthony McHale, S. J., and Horace McKenna, S. J.,
who tried to see God in each of us.

Contents

Introduction

Abraham Lincoln probably never stepped foot into Gonzaga College or its adjacent St. Patrick's Church. The thirteenth president was not a Catholic, not even a traditionally religious man. But when a .44 bullet from John W. Booth's derringer pierced Lincoln's brain, the lives of many Gonzaga families quickly intersected with Lincoln's in innumerable ways.

The murder certainly ranked as one of the most traumatic events in the city. Yet when researching the subject for a previous book about Gonzaga, *Echo Ever Proudly: Gonzaga College High School in the Press 1821-1899*, I found only a handful of these intersections and connections between the school and the assassination, and most in an unusual way — in anti-Catholic books and web sites.

Indeed, a history composed to honor Gonzaga's diamond jubilee in 1896 had but one slight reference to the whole matter. When referring to Gonzaga's President Bernardin Wiget, S. J., that volume states "his name became national on account of his spiritual ministrations to the poor woman who suffered on the scaffold for the crimes of others."

That diamond jubilee history focused mostly on Gonzaga's internal history and the Jesuits who ran the school, but in 1921, even with another quarter-century of perspective, a centennial history again fails to get into the subject. It repeats the above quotation, though noting the poor woman was "Mrs. Surratt."

Both volumes note that Wiget left little work documenting his administration or the assassination. Perhaps the latter was too painful or he was simply too busy running a college, a parish and serving as a Union chaplain to wounded soldiers. Or perhaps the involvement of several Catholics in the assassination convinced him to simply attend to his Breviary. But if the Jesuit's intent was just to let the matter go, a surprising thing happened in 1883, when the matter was still fresh. In publishing its alumni directory, the school compilers efficiently but perhaps unintentionally listed one David E. Herold, the Lincoln assassin hung for his crime and Gonzaga's most infamous alumnus. Yet they didn't even put an asterisk next to his name indicating he was dead. All the above leaves far more questions than answers.

Something the Jesuits who compiled those two limited Gonzaga histories did not have, however, was the Internet, which, when used with the list of Gonzaga alumni and their addresses, newspaper digitization and the new Google book search, has given you much of the monograph you have before you. Photos from the Library of Congress online were invaluable too. Add to that the tremendous research done by individuals for the Surratt Society and certain key authors, like Michael Kauffman, Roy Chamlee, Jr., Elizabeth Trindal and James Swanson. My Internet-based research pales in comparison with theirs undertaken in the stacks and microfilm rooms of the National Archives and Library of Congress.

But like all Lincoln authors, I was able to immerse myself in the times, something once compared to the diver's rapture of the deep. Often I felt quite present in 1865 and at the old Gonzaga College located between 9th and 10th Sts. on F, just around the corner from Ford's Theater. Helping me along those rutted, muddy thoroughfares were a host of people: Mike Dolan, my Gonzaga classmate, author, and Renaissance man; my wife, Katherine Norton Warren, a superb writer, proofreader and cheerleader; my brother, Dr. Daniel Warren, Ph. D. (Class of 1972) and son Dr. Christopher Norton Warren, D. Phil., (Class of 1995), both of whom brought keen editorial eyes to my writing. Extremely helpful also was assassination historian Michael Kauffman, who kindly read and corrected my manuscript and inspired me through his superb research for *American Brutus* and other works. Also, I'm grateful to Greg Jones and Debbie Jacobs for help in preparing the manuscript for publication, as well as to Sean Maloney, reference librarian at Siena College, for training his editorial eye on the final version. Thanks too to the Gonzaga Development Office, which prepared the wonderful covers, including the back cover which shows how the Gonzaga wheelbarrow may have looked.

Photos are courtesy of, among others, the Library of Congress; the Surratt Society; the Lincoln Museum in Ft. Wayne, Indiana; James Swanson and Daniel Weinberg, authors of *Lincoln's Assassins: Their Trial and Execution* and Thomas Bradley.

All proceeds from the sale of this book go to Gonzaga College High School.

1

The People and The Places

David E. Herold (Gonzaga student in 1858), convicted in assassination and hanged.[1]

Louis Weichmann (1849), boarder at house of convicted and hanged assassin Mary Surratt and one of two key government witnesses against the plotters.[2] Weichmann, who once met Lincoln,[3] was a friend of the Petersen family, in whose house Lincoln died[4] and from which he saw soldiers remove Lincoln's casket.[5]

The Rev. Bernardin Wiget, S. J., president of Gonzaga College, confessor to Mary Surratt,[6] and one-time teacher of her sons,[7] including charged conspirator John Surratt. Wiget once met with Lincoln in the White House.

John P. Brophy, teacher at Gonzaga[8] and St. Aloysius,[9] who led efforts to save Mary Surratt from the gallows by attacking Weichmann's testimony. He married a grand-niece of President Tyler.[10]

Henri Benjamin St. Marie, former Gonzaga teacher[11] who served in the Papal Guard in Rome and identified fellow guard John Surratt as the escaped assassin. John Surratt was later tried separately from his mother Mary but was freed when the jury deadlocked.

Dr. John Frederick May (1826), one of the physicians who treated the dying Lincoln.[12] He also identified the dead body of John Wilkes Booth, who had been a patient.[13] May's brother, Henry

(1826), was a Congressman from Maryland who, during House debate, opposed Lincoln, whom he said had "overthrown...our freedom of speech, our liberty of the press, our private property, our personal liberty...our personal security." Their father was physician to President William Harrison, and their grandfather took part in the Boston Tea Party.

Dr. Samuel Mudd, convicted, imprisoned and pardoned conspirator and grandfather of Dr. Richard Mudd (1917). Dr. Richard Mudd spent his long life (he lived to be 101) working to clear his grandfather's name. He and his family obtained strong personal support from Presidents Carter and Reagan but ultimately failed in Federal Court. Some modern historians believe Mudd conspired in the planned abduction but not the assassination.[14]

Joseph H. Bradley (1824), chief defense counsel for John Surratt. Asked earlier to represent David Herold, he declined.[15]

Judge George P. Fisher, father of Charles (1864), judge in trial of John Surratt. Judge Fisher was appointed a judge by Lincoln after completing a term as a congressman from Delaware. Fisher and Joseph Bradley fought so bitterly during the John Surratt trial that Fisher disbarred Bradley after the judge contended Bradley physically threatened him. Fisher also commanded the Union's 3rd Delaware Regiment in which Henri St. Marie served after teaching at Gonzaga and prior to turning in Surratt.[16]

Richard T. Merrick, brother of William Merrick (1824), who joined Bradley in defending John Surratt at his separate assassination trial. The Merricks were nephews of Rev. William Mathews, Gonzaga's second president, the man who gave the Jesuits the land to build the first Gonzaga (then called Washington Catholic Seminary), between 9th and 10th Sts. on F St., near Ford's Theater. Richard Merrick declined to represent accused assassin Dr. Samuel Mudd, though he quietly offered Mudd's attorney advice in the case.

John A. W. Clarvoe, father of John T. Clarvoe (1870), Washington police detective and the first officer to reach the scene of the assassination. He was first to go to the Surratt boarding house and also searched for the assassins in southern Maryland.[17]

Honora Fitzpatrick, sister of Peter P. Fitzpatrick (1848), 19-year-old boarder at Mary Surratt's boarding house. She and Mary Surratt's daughter, Anna, were friends and the two were smitten with John Wilkes Booth. They bought photos of the handsome actor, and when Anna hid one behind a picture frame, its discovery by police added to a sense of guilt in the household.

John F. Coyle, father of Frank Coyle (1865), editor of the *National Intelligencer*, who allegedly was given or was to be given a letter by John Wilkes Booth before the assassination, presumably a justification for Booth's impending actions. He spoke with Booth the day of the killing. Coyle had known Booth's father and the younger Booth since the latter was a child.[18] Coyle, an investor in Ford's Theater, had bailed out theater carpenter James Gifford after he was arrested as a suspect. Gifford had helped build the Booth family home near Baltimore.[19]

Maj. Thomas Donoho, father of George (1851), colleague of Coyle at the *National Intelligencer* who was with Coyle at that sidewalk encounter with Booth the day of the assassination. Donoho had known Booth's father.[20]

Richard Wallach (1822), mayor of Washington, D.C., who after the shooting attempted to calm potential rioters at the theater.[21] He rode the funeral train that carried Lincoln's remains to Springfield.[22]

Hugh B. Sweeny (1824), father of George (1854), next door neighbor to Mary Surratt's H St. boarding house. Sweeny, a banker, was instrumental in the 1853 sale of the house to Mary's husband.[23]

Dr. Francis S. Walsh, father of Joseph (1865) and Redmond Daniel (1875), a druggist with whom David Herold boarded for 11 months while working as a druggist at Walsh's pharmacy.[24]

Gen. James A. Hardie, father of Francis and Joseph (both 1869), and Assistant Secretary of War. Hardie served as intermediary between the government and Mary Surratt's confessors and was involved in a major contretemps after allegedly placing restrictions on whether one of the priests could publicly declare Surratt innocent.[25]

Gen. Thomas Ewing, brother of Brig. Gen. Charles Bernard Ewing (1849), was defense counsel to the convicted Dr. Samuel Mudd, Samuel Arnold and Edman Spangler. Their cousin, lawyer Britten Hill, helped investigate the shooting while Lincoln lay dying in another room of the Petersen house.

Thompson Nailor, father of Notley Nailor (1865), owned the livery stable from which, the night of the assassination, David Herold rented and then stole a horse. Booth boarded horses at Nailor's as part of the plot. Notley Nailor was the school's top student leader that year.

Gen. Montgomery Meigs, brother-in-law of John Rodgers (1824), who secured with troops the Petersen House where Lincoln died[26] and sat through the night with the President. Rodgers' father in 1831 had built and occupied the house at which Herold and Powell attempted to kill Secretary of State Seward.

Charles Gautier, father of Peter Gautier (1852), owner of Gautier's Restaurant at 252 Pennsylvania Ave., site of a raucous, drunken late-night gathering of the plotters as they debated how to kidnap Lincoln. Gautier had catered Lincoln's Inaugural Ball.

Catherine J. Gautier, sister of Peter, who married Capt. Edward P. Doherty. Doherty led the cavalry troops who found and killed Booth and captured Herold and brought them back to Washington.

William A. Harlan (1868), brother-in-law of Robert Todd Lincoln, Abraham Lincoln's son. William's sister, Mary, married Robert Lincoln in 1868.

Adele Cutts Douglas, step-mother of Stephen (1859) and Robert (1859) and niece of Walter Cutts (1821) and Thomas Cutts (1821), and widow of Ill. Sen. Stephen Douglas, who ran against Lincoln for the Presidency. She made the final personal appeal to President Johnson seeking clemency for Mrs. Surratt.[27] She was the model for St. Aloysius Gonzaga's mother in the Constantine Brumidi painting above the altar at St. Aloysius Church on Capitol Hill.

Benjamin Ogle Tayloe, brother of Henry (1825) and Charles (1825), among the wealthiest men in Washington at the time and speculated to be a possible espionage mastermind behind plans to abduct Lincoln.[28]

Elisabeth Quesenberry, whose sister had married into the Tayloe family, operated a safe house for Confederates across the Potomac in Virginia. It was here Booth and Herold sought refuge after escaping from Maryland.[29]

John F. Callan, father of Charles (1851), sought to get Mrs. Surratt spared from the gallows and notarized statements by John Brophy that Weichmann had lied. John's father was chief overseer for construction of the White House.

Effie Germon, sister-in-law of artist Constantine Brumidi. She was an actress whose picture was one of four found on Booth's body.[30] Brumidi painted St. Aloysius' murals at its time of construction and those at the Capitol. Effie Germon was one of Brumidi's painting models.

George Washington Riggs, father of Elisha (1865), and founder of Riggs Bank. He built the Riggs Mansion at what became the Soldiers' Home, while the mansion became Lincoln's summer White House. Booth and his co-conspirators unsuccessfully tried to abduct the President on the road there. Lincoln once was shot at by an unknown assailant en route to that estate. Lincoln's primary residence, the White House, was designed and built by James Hoban, who designed the original Gonzaga and sent his son to school there. George Washington Riggs was also close to the family of Major Henry Rathbone, who shared the fateful box with the Lincolns the night of the murder and was stabbed by Booth. Rathbone's son, who became a Congressman, was named Henry Riggs Rathbone. Abraham Lincoln personally banked at Riggs.

Randolph Coyle, father of John Coyle (1851), the surveyor who diagrammed Ford's Theater for the prosecution at the assassins' trial.[31]

Charles and Joseph Gawler (both 1865), with their father, Joseph, served as undertakers for the reinterred remains of assassins Herold and Powell.[32]

J.M. Carlisle (1826), Washington attorney, asked by David Herold to represent him at his trial. Carlisle had refused to take an oath of allegiance to the Union at the beginning of the war and thus could not practice before the Military Commission or any other Court in Washington except the U.S. Supreme Court.[33]

The Rev. Charles Stonestreet, S.J., Gonzaga president 1858-59, who testified as to Mary Surratt's character at her trial. Stonestreet taught Dr. Mudd at a Jesuit school in Frederick, Maryland[34] and baptized Mary Surratt's two nieces and mother-in-law.[35]

The Rev. L. Roccofort, S.J., St. Aloysius associate pastor and confessor to Louis Weichmann. Called to testify at the trial of John Surratt, Roccofort was asked if Weichmann, outside of confession, had told the priest he had supplied information to the Confederacy. The Court barred Roccofort from answering but Weichmann bitterly felt Roccofort had left the impression Weichmann had done just that.[36]

Thomas Jenkins (1854), nephew of Mary Surratt.

William Wallach (1822), owner of the *Washington Star*, which chronicled the assassination and trial. He was brother of Richard Wallach, the city's mayor.

Maj. John F. Lee, father of William and Arthur (both 1856) and first cousin of Confederate Gen. Robert. E. Lee. John Lee was adjutant general of the Union Army until 1862, when he resigned. His successor, Gen. Joseph Holt, was chief prosecutor at the trial of the conspirators, a job Lee theoretically could have held had he remained. Another Lee cousin, Confederate Brig. Gen. Edwin Gray Lee, assumed command of Canadian covert operations in the fall of 1864, when plans to abduct Lincoln were being discussed. Lee ordered John Surratt to spy on a Union prison camp in Elmira, N.Y., which is where Surratt contended he was during the assassination.[37]

Lieut. Otway Berryman (1822), a naval explorer who took soundings in the Atlantic Ocean that directly led to the laying of the new trans-Atlantic telegraph cable.[38] One of very first transmissions announced the first of John Surratt's two arrests, this at the Vatican.

Commodore Louis M. Goldsborough, brother of Commodore John R. Goldsborough (1821). John Surratt, after being captured in Egypt, was delivered to Goldsborough's flagship in Marseilles where, Surratt said in an April 3, 1898 *Washington Post* article, Louis Goldsborough sympathetically saw him as "only a beardless boy."

Frederick Weichmann (1850), brother of Louis who became a parish priest in Anderson, Indiana. Louis moved to be with him and opened a business school there.

Sites with Gonzaga Associations

Kirkwood House hotel, once owned by family of Albert R. Kirkwood and John H. Kirkwood (both 1863). The Pennsylvania Ave. hotel was residence of Vice President Johnson, sworn in as President there after Lincoln expired. Johnson's assigned assassin, George Atzerodt, had taken the room above Johnson but fled instead of killing him. It was here also that Booth, who at times stayed at the hotel, left a cryptic note for Johnson asking if he was in.

Herndon Hotel at the corner of 9th and F Sts., was where plotter Lewis Powell roomed and where the other conspirators formally decided to kill Lincoln April 14. Powell was on the third floor and in a corner room[39] looking out onto F St. and Gonzaga. Fooled -- or perhaps cooperating -- into obtaining the room for him was Anna Ward, a teacher at the Visitation School for Girls, next to Gonzaga. Attending that school was Apollonia Dean, a 10-year-old, who boarded at the Surratt boarding house.

Willard Hotel, owned by the Willard Family [Caleb (1849); Stephen (1849); Everett (1865); Edwin (1868)], was where Gen. Ulysses Grant stayed the night before the assassination. News that the Grants were to join the Lincolns at Ford's that night prompted the assassins' decision to act in hopes of killing both. David Herold at one point may have been assigned to kill Grant.

Carusi's Saloon, owned by family of Nathaniel, Francis and John (all 1858) was to be site of a speech by John Surratt about his role in the planned abduction of Lincoln. Tumultuous opposition to the speech resulted in it being cancelled.[40]

St. Aloysius Church, site of organ and music recitals that drew John Wilkes Booth and John Surratt. The program from one of these recitals was confiscated by police from Mrs. Surratt. At one of these recitals, Booth made a $5 contribution to the parish.[41]

Ford's Theater was the site of the July 6, 1864 Gonzaga College Commencement exercises.

Notes

[1] *Gonzaga College Registration and Alumni Records* (Washington, D.C.).

[2] All alumni are identified through Gonzaga's Registration and Alumni records in its Archives and/or those in the Georgetown University Archives. Parents, siblings and others are identified through these records, those of the 1860 and 1870 censuses and the *1865 City Directory* on microfiche at the Washington Historical Society, *Eliot's Washington Directory of 1827 and Hunter's Washington and Georgetown Directory of 1853*. (Washington, D.C.). The year a student attended Gonzaga (e. g. 1823) is from an 1883 directory of known past students (see back of this book) and/or original registration records. It does not indicate whether or not a student graduated from the

school, which is not as common as it is today, or how long he attended. Also, until the establishment of quality Catholic, private and public elementary schools in the District in the 1850s and 1860s, students as young as eight and as old as their early twenties would enroll at Gonzaga.

[3] Louis J. Weichmann and Floyd E. Risvold, ed., *A True History of the Assassination of Abraham Lincoln and of the Conspiracy of 1865* (New York: Vintage Books, 1977) 6. Weichmann spelled his first name both Louis and Lewis and his last name both Weichmann and Wiechmann.

[4] Weichmann, *A True History,* p. 12.

[5] Weichmann, *A True History,* p. 180.

[6] *Woodstock Letters* of Md. Jesuit Province, Vol. 12, p. 192-93. Obituary with reference to Lincoln meeting, also.

[7] Elizabeth Steger Trindal, *Mary Surratt, An American Tragedy* (Gretna, LA: Pelican Publishing Co., 1996) 42; hereafter cited as *MSAAT.*

[8] Trindal, *MSAAT,* p. 255, Note 26A.

[9] *Daily Constitutional Union* 5 Sept 1865: 3.

[10] *New York Sun* 22 Feb 1914: 15.

[11] *New York Tribune* 20 May 1867: 5; reprinted in *Surratt Society Courier* Aug 1991 (Clinton, Maryland).

[12] Michael Kauffman, *American Brutus: John Wilkes Booth and the Lincoln Conspiracies* (New York: Random House, 2004) 46.

[13] Kauffman, *American Brutus,* p. 323.

[14] Edward Steers, Jr., et al., *The Trial: The Assassination of President Lincoln and the Trial of the Conspirators* (Lexington: The University Press of Kentucky, 2003) LXXIX-LXXXVII; hereafter cited as *TTTAPLTC.*

[15] Roy Z. Chamlee, Jr., *Lincoln's Assassins: A Complete Account of Their Capture, Trial, and Punishment* (North Carolina: McFarland & Co., 1990) 219.

[16] Weichmann, *A True History,* p. 24

[17] Kauffman, *American Brutus,* pp. 18, 75.

[18] Weichmann, *A True History,* p. 138.

[19] *Surratt Society Courier* April 1994: I-43, I-44 and *Washington Post* 22 June 1878: 1; 30 Mar 1902: 35.

[20] Weichmann, *A True History,* p. 138

[21] J. E. Buckingham, Sr., *Reminiscences and Souvenirs Of The Assassination of Abraham Lincoln* (Washington: Press of Rufus H. Darby, 1904) 15.

[22] *Washington Star* Undated: April 1865: clipping.

[23] Trindal, *MSAAT,* p.82.

[24] Edward Steers, Jr., ed., *TTTAPLTC,* p. 96.

[25] Kauffman, *American Brutus,* p. 376.

[26] Furguson, Ernest B., *Freedom Rising* (New York: Vintage Books, 2004), 383.

[27] Chamlee, *Lincoln's Assassins*, p. 465.

[28] William A. Tidwell, James O. Hall and David Winfred Gaddy, *Come Retribution: The Confederate Secret Service and the Assassination of Lincoln* (Jackson: The University Press of Mississippi, 1988) 273; hereafter cited as *CRTCSSAL*.

[29] Tidwell, *CRTCSSAL*, p. 457.

[30] Kauffman, *American Brutus*, p. 462, Note 1.

[31] *Washington Post* 30 March 1902: 35.

[32] *The Evening Star* 15 Feb 1869: n.pag. and *The Washington Post* 12 June 1994: n.pag.

[33] Chamlee, *Lincoln's Assassins*, p. 219.

[34] Steers, Jr., ed., *TTTAPLTC*, p. 213.

[35] Trindal, *MSAAT*, p. 173.

[36] Weichmann, *True History*, pp. 376, 377.

[37] Tidwell, *CRTCSSAL*, p. 430.

[38] Chester Hearn, *Circuits in the Sea: The Men, The Ships and the Atlantic Cable* (New Hampshire: Greenwood Publishing Group 2004), 20.

[39] Paul Warren, Correspondence with Michael Kauffman re: *American Brutus* (n.p.: n.p., n.d.) n. pag.

[40] Chamlee, *Lincoln's Assassins*, p. 537.

[41] Surratt Society records, notes of James O. Hall re St. Aloysius Church.

David Herold (Gonzaga 1858) shortly after his capture while leading John Wilkes Booth to Virginia.

Louis Weichmann (1849) was a boarder in the house of Mary Surratt and her son, John. He became a prime witness against them both.

Rev. Bernardin Wiget, S.J., president of Gonzaga College, confessor to Mary Surratt and one-time teacher of her sons. Wiget stood by Mary Surratt on the gallows.

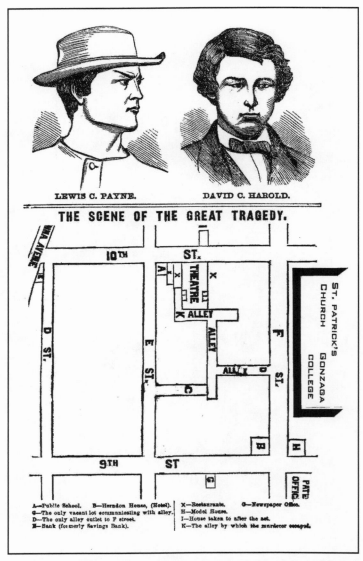

Contemporary illustration of the area around Ford's Theater. Location of Gonzaga and St. Patrick's were added for this book. Lewis Payne was actually named Lewis Powell.

Gonzaga College, between 9th and 10th Sts. on F.

St. Patrick's Church, adjacent to Gonzaga College on far right.

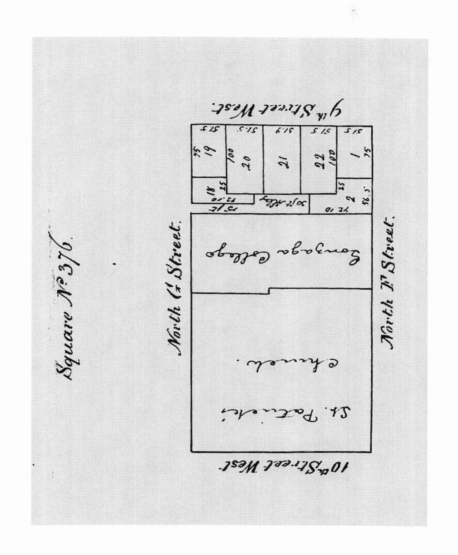

Photo of F St. about 1870. At the center of the photo is the Herndon House hotel, where the plotters met in the 3rd floor corner room. Directly across the street is the Masonic Temple, and next to it, just peeking out, are Gonzaga and St. Patrick's.

Ford's Theater draped in black right after the assassination. Only nine months earlier, Gonzaga had held commencement exercises here.

Contemporary illustration of Herold being held as the mortally wounded Booth is dragged from a burning Virginia barn.

A similar illustration of the Herold capture and Booth shooting.

2

A Priest, His Penitent and His Pupils

Father Bernardin Wiget, S. J., stood atop the gallows. Fifteen steps above the small crowd, the president of Gonzaga College no doubt struggled with feelings of anger, shame and sadness. Two of his own stood with him on that grim platform that day, both convicted in the murder of Abraham Lincoln, both about to die.

One was David Herold, a young man who had attended Gonzaga College, the Jesuit school that Wiget ran. The other was a middle-aged woman, Mary Surratt, a worshiper at St. Aloysius, Wiget's church, and a friend of long standing.[1]

The temperature that July 7 was 100°, and the sun, like military justice, was merciless. This was no weather for black clothing, yet that was what the priest and his parishioner wore. Wiget stood by the seated Surratt as she kissed a crucifix. The bespectacled Jesuit tried without success to ease the doomed woman's terror. A minister attended to Herold, an Episcopalian, who also had the look of one about to hang.

By 1865 war had swelled Washington's population census to some 200,000. The city throbbed with the energy such times and such influxes generate. Troops bivouacked on the grounds of the White House and the Capitol. The army had seized buildings for use as hospitals. A decaying brick structure on Capitol Hill, called "the Old Capitol" because it was where the Congress had convened after the British burned the Capitol in 1814, was now a federal prison. The city's graveyards had filled to capacity. Saloons, restaurants, houses of prostitution and gambling halls lined streets that were often packed with military men.[2]

Those military men were not always in uniform, and they weren't always with the Union. A common language and an extremely porous border between the United States of America and the Confederate States of America, particularly along the Potomac River south of Washington, D.C., meant that southern spies, profiteering blockade runners, and the merely curious could and did visit the Union capital.

Only five years earlier, Washington had been home to a mere 60,000, a fourth the size of nearby Baltimore. Neighbor knew neighbor. The baker knew the butcher. The Senators knew the Mayor. Even then full of transients, Washington nonetheless was in those days also a home town, a genuine community that educated youngsters and saw to residents' spiritual wellbeing. And at the confluence of the educational and spiritual worlds stood school and church. For the city's Roman Catholics, those pillars were Gonzaga College at 917 F St., the adjacent St. Patrick's Church, and St. Aloysius, the new Jesuit church in Swampoodle, north of the Capitol. The school (which attracted plenty of non-Catholics) and the parishes, one long established, the other new, were hubs of the city's Catholic life.

So it is no wonder that on that terrible Good Friday of April 14, 1865, Abraham Lincoln's assassination drew scores of Gonzaga alumni, faculty, students and parents into an intricate web of circumstance that illustrates the social history of the time.

It was a time when American society was asked to choose north or south, blue or grey, Union or Confederacy. In the years before, during and after the Civil War, Gonzaga and Catholic Washington indeed had leaned strongly to the south.

Among the earliest Catholics to come to North America from Europe had been a contingent from England that colonized what became St. Mary's County, Maryland. From there the faith spread through southern Maryland and what would become Washington, D.C.

In the counties around Washington, the righteousness of slaveholding and the gospel of State's Rights were taught with the ABCs.

Whatever their stands on such matters, in the days leading to the Civil War, Washington area Jesuits were ordered to keep political talk to a minimum and even ordered not to vote. Some of these Jesuits, like their Southern students, stood with the Confederacy, at least in principle. A Jesuit who served at Gonzaga reported in his diary that Fr. Wiget, for one, had disagreed with a French Bishop who declared slavery immoral. Southern Catholic clergy had argued that slavery was affirmed in the Bible.[3]

At about 10:15 p.m. on Good Friday, John Wilkes Booth snuck into the Presidential box behind the laughing President and First Lady, enjoying "Our American Cousin." He aimed his single shot .44 caliber derringer, and, timing his firing to coincide with the show's most raucous laugh, pulled the trigger and shot Abraham Lincoln in the brain. Booth stabbed a Union officer who tried unsuccessfully to stop him from jumping to the stage, where Booth landed awkwardly, perhaps injuring his leg. Declared the melodramatic Booth: "Sic Semper Tyrannis."

Within seconds, he had fled through the theater's back door where an unsuspecting stagehand stood obligingly holding his horse. He grabbed the reins and wildly fled up the alley opening that led onto F St. Directly ahead of the assassin as he thundered up that narrow passage stood Gonzaga, the ivied grey brick college opened in 1821. It's doubtful any of the 13 Jesuits living at the school noticed the clatter Booth raised along F St. as he whipped his horse. It was Good Friday. Silent prayer, services or sleep were required of the disciplined Order.

But within minutes, the Jesuits would have been looking out the windows. A riot was erupting. Word of the shooting had spread like a wave. Terror filled the streets, a spasm of fear such as would grip Washington again on September 11, 2001. An agreement had been signed at Appomattox, but could the Confederates be staging an insurgency that started with the murder of the man who had defeated them? Had someone really bludgeoned Secretary William Seward in his sickbed? Was the vice president slain? Was Washington about to burn, as had Sherman's Atlanta?

Thousands of newly surrendered and uniformed Rebels roamed the capital. Suddenly, each posed a threat.

Bluecoats and civilians alike screamed for Confederate heads. The streets vibrated with rumors and fear. As crowds jammed the area around 10th and F Sts., between Gonzaga and Ford's Theater, police and soldiers called repeatedly for order, to no avail. Mayor Richard Wallach (a Gonzaga student in 1824) spoke, trying to pacify the mob.[4] But the president lay dying in the Petersen House across from Ford's. And the citizenry would not be soothed.

As the human tide surged and the president's life ebbed, Secretary of War Edwin Stanton began the hard business of investigation, conducting interviews in the Petersen House to identify the killers. John Wilkes Booth was the first identified. The actor's was one of the nation's most famous faces, and few could mistake that it was he who had made the dramatic leap onto the stage after the shooting.

One of the first to hear Booth had co-conspirators was John A. W. Clarvoe (Parent of Gonzaga student in 1870), a Washington police detective and the first officer to reach the scene of the shooting.[5] An informant told Clarvoe that a John Surratt, living at 541 (now 604) H St. was known to associate with Booth. At about 1 a.m. Saturday morning Clarvoe and other detectives rang the doorbell at the

Washington Mayor Richard Wallach (1822) was called upon to try and calm rioters at Ford's after the shooting. The mayor also rode the Lincoln funeral train to Illinois.

Kirkwood House Hotel, where one of the plotters stayed. He was assigned to kill Vice President Johnson. Ironically, Johnson was sworn into office here. The hotel had been owned by the family of Albert R. and John H. Kirkwood (both 1863).

Surratt residence. Louis Weichmann (1849), a boarder who lived on the second floor, got up half-dressed and came down the stairs.

Weichmann, 23, clerked in the War Department. He and his two brothers had been educated at Gonzaga, where Louis won top academic prizes in classics, arithmetic and French. He and his brothers had been enrolled by their parents after the family moved from Philadelphia. Weichmann's stiff, formal demeanor would have suited him well in the classroom but not in the F St. schoolyard. In addition to his other academic achievements at Gonzaga, Weichmann won honors for Christian Doctrine,[6] which perhaps contributed to his decision, after completing high school in Philadelphia, to enroll for a time at St. Charles Borromeo in Ellicott City, Maryland. St. Charles was a pre-seminary for aspiring priests. There the pious and studious Weichmann had become fast friends with fellow would-be seminarian John Surratt, a connection that, to Weichmann's dismay, would last the rest of his life.

Weichmann answered the door.

"Who is there?" he asked.

"Detectives," a voice said from the other side of the door. "Is John Surratt in?"

"No sir," said Weichmann. "He is not in the city."

The policemen insisted on talking to Surratt's mother. Weichmann went to wake Mrs. Surratt, leaving the door ajar. The detectives walked through unbidden. Mrs. Surratt came down. Detective Clarvoe asked about her son.

"John is not in the city, sir," Mary Surratt said, adding that it had been almost two weeks since she last had seen him.

Room by room, the detectives roused the Surratt household, talking with all 13 inhabitants. Weichmann quietly escorted the policemen until he could stand it no more.

"Will you be kind enough to tell me the meaning of all this?" the clerk said.

"That is a pretty question for you to ask me," Clarvoe said. "Where have you been tonight?"

"I have been here in the house."

"Have you been here all evening?" one of the policemen asked.

"No, I have been down in the country with Mrs. Surratt," Weichmann replied.

"Do you pretend to tell me you have not heard the President has been murdered?" asked Clarvoe.

"Great God," Weichmann said dumbfounded, adding cryptically, "I see it all now."

Clarvoe produced a black bow tie, stained red.

"Do you see the blood on that?" he said. "This is the blood of Abraham Lincoln. John Wilkes Booth did that and I suppose John Surratt has assassinated the Secretary of State."

Weichmann hurried downstairs to the front parlor where his landlady stood.

"Mrs. Surratt, what do you think, Booth has murdered the President," he said.

"My God, Mr. Weichmann, you do not tell me so," Mrs. Surratt replied.[7] She should have been less worried about what Weichmann was telling her than what her favorite boarder would be telling others. But Mrs. Surratt was a woman who by now was used to boarders, friends and relatives alike gossiping about her bad luck and terrible choice in a husband.

Mary Elizabeth Jenkins Surratt was born in 1823 on a farm in Prince Georges County, Maryland, the daughter of Archibald and Elizabeth Anne Jenkins, who also had two sons. The family practiced the Anglican faith. By the time the girl was two years old, her father was dead. It was a struggle, but the widow Jenkins managed to hold onto the family farm and its 11 slaves, as well as buy more land. When Mary was 12, her mother sent her to the Academy for Young Ladies, affiliated with St. Mary's Catholic Church in Alexandria, Virginia. The school was operated by the Daughters of Charity.[8] But St. Mary's was a Jesuit parish. Mary's enrollment at the academy began a long association for her and the Order, a factor that helped persuade her to convert to Catholicism.

Perhaps because she'd never known her father, Mary married young. In 1840, at 17, she wed John Harrison Surratt, 26, a drab farmer and mill owner. The two lived in a small frame house a stone's throw from the grist mill John ran at Oxon Run in Prince George's County.

Mary Surratt.

John Surratt.

Mary Surratt's boarding house on H St. Boarding there were her son, John, once a pupil of Gonzaga President Wiget in southern Maryland, and Louis Weichmann (1849), a prime witness against the conspirators. Wiget was Mrs. Surratt's confessor and appears to have visited the boarding house the day after the assassination. Wiget that day saw to it that a wheelbarrow marked "Gonzaga" was removed from the house, presumably through the door on the lower left. It had been loaned to Mrs. Surratt by the school. The house on one side was the residence of banker Hugh Sweeny (1824), who helped sell the boarding house to the Surratt family.

In 1841 Mary gave birth to a son, Isaac. Daughter Elizabeth Suzannah, known as Anna, came in 1843. John arrived in April 1844. Life was not easy with Surratt, a stubborn, sometimes angry man known to take more than one drink. Along with raising her children, Mary channeled her energies into the construction of a neighborhood church in nearby Oxon Hill. St. Ignatius would become another of the area's Jesuit parishes, which also included St. Thomas Manor in Chapel Point.

The first priest to serve at St. Ignatius was Rev. Joseph Finotti, S. J., with whom Mary felt a strong bond. Father Finotti, who had emigrated from Italy, offered advice on many matters, as well as comfort to a deeply religious mother-of-three alienated from her husband.

The 1850 dedication of St. Ignatius doubtless raised Mary's spirits, but her life took a harsh turn. The next year, the Surratt home went up in flames. The suspected arsonist was an angry slave.

The Surratts moved in with Mary's cousin, Thomas Jenkins, his wife, Charity, and their six children. Instead of rebuilding the burned dwelling, John Surratt decided to build and operate a combination residence and roadhouse at the intersection of Washington-Port Tobacco and Marlboro-Piscataway roads. The town that developed there became known as Surrattsville. Later, out of shame, it would be renamed Clinton. The nine-room building still stands at 9118 Brandywine Rd.

Surratt got the structure up and opened the tavern. In 1853 the family moved in. John Surratt, however, also had his eye on a growing Washington, D.C. Having sold most of his lands to build his tavern, he took what funds he did have to buy a rooming house on H St. in the capital city through Hugh Sweeney (1824). Within a year, Mary was seeking help coping with her alcoholic husband. In a letter to Father Finotti, she wrote that she had not spoken with Surratt in nearly two weeks. Writing of a particular night, she complained: "I thought that I would see if he intended to retire or not. His company had all left him and he was spread out at his full length beastly drunk in the bar room." She also wanted to enroll Anna in a Catholic boarding school. Once she had Anna placed in St. Mary's Female Institute in nearby Bryantown, Mary needed help with sons Isaac, 14, and John, 11.

On Dec. 30, 1854, the Rev. L. Nota, S. J., of Georgetown College, the Jesuit institution perched on a hill west of the old port that now is part of the nation's capital, took the stage at the Surratt tavern. He was performing a baptism nearby. Taking the circuit-riding Jesuit aside, Mary Surratt told Fr. Nota of her concern for her boys. She asked his help in getting her sons out of the tavern and into a school. Nota wrote to Rev. Bernardin Wiget, S. J., president of a new school at St. Thomas Manor in nearby Chapel Point, where Anna had made her first communion.

In his Jan. 3, 1855 missive, Nota wrote to Wiget:

I have been last Saturday as near to you as Bryantown is, but owing to the want of time and of a conveyance, I could not have the pleasure to pay you visit according to my wishes. I hope you have spent the Christmas holy days in good health [...] and with the great profit of the mission as usual. While in Bryantown I baptized two girls [...] they expect to make their first communion at Easter next, and it is expected you will be kind enough to see to that [...] There is at the Institution [St. Mary's], a daughter of Mrs. Surratt, a very interesting girl, and has made her first communion at your hand. Her mother, living in Prince George's County, wishes her to be recommended to you and besides begs a favor for her two sons that are still at home: viz., that with your known liberality you will have them both, or either of the two, taught at your school as cheap as you can afford. The reason of her begging for such a favor (which she has never done in her life) is, because her husband not being a Catholic and having suffered severe losses, is unable to give them a decent education, but the mother, an excellent Catholic, and very much attached to us, is very anxious to raise them well: her means, however, are very limited, as she is obliged (in consequence of the aforesaid losses) to keep a public house, where the public stage stops but occasionally.

So you see that this lady, Mrs. Mary Surratt, is worth all we can possibly [do] for her and her children. She is a real Lady, but in distress and begs a favor for the sake of religion. I hope you will grant the request.

Whilst at her house, I promised her to write to you & afterwards to let her know your decision either to board & teach them altogether gratuitously, or at least, for how much you would do so; and if you could not board them, where they could safely be boarded and for how much. I would suggest the house of Mr. Stone or some other family like that one. But you know better by yourself.

This is the first favor I beg of you for a pious cause. I expect you will not refuse it entirely, chiefly considering how much God helps you and your endeavors, not only in spiritualibus but in temporalibus also. My compliments to all the fathers, brothers & friends there.

Please to answer as is convenient, and believe me to be
Your dev. Serv. & Brother.
L. Nota, S.J.

Father Wiget remembered the Surratts from Anna's First Communion in 1854, when he had been dividing his time between the school and the parish at Chapel Point.

Ordained a Jesuit only four years before and himself new to the rural school, Wiget could not enroll the Surratt boys at St. Thomas without permission from his Jesuit superior, Rev. Charles Stonestreet, S. J. Stonestreet was a veteran Jesuit educator who had taught at Georgetown College and St. John's College in Frederick, Maryland. One of his charges at both schools was Samuel Mudd, a Prince George's native who had gone on to practice medicine in the county.

Writing to Stonestreet on the Surratt boys' behalf, Wiget sent along Nota's communiqué to buttress his case for enrolling the sons.

I enclose a letter of Fr. Nota: examine the request he makes. I am perfectly willing to be kind, as kind as possible, being mindful of 'date and datibus vobis.' I could not obtain for the two boys anything from my neighbors except, maybe, cheap lodging. I could board them & in case of necessity could also lodge them, but do not think would be justified to do more than to reduce three terms to the half, viz., to

$58.50 per ten months, provided the boys be well behaved boys and above 14 years of age. I thought of a charity boarder in the very beginning of our school & feel inclined to think God would bless for it. Yes, as I write it here I leave all to your decision. Please give an answer to Fr. Nota ...
Pray for me ... Yr humble son in Christ
Bernardin Wiget, S. J.

Stonestreet agreed to the proposal, and the Surratt boys enrolled at St. Thomas.

In 1867, testifying at the John Surratt's trial in the Lincoln assassination plot, Father Wiget, then president of Gonzaga, was asked how long he had known the accused conspirator.

The Rev. Charles Stonestreet, S. J., Gonzaga president 1858-59, who testified as to Mary Surratt's character at her trial. He had taught convicted conspirator Samuel Mudd in Frederick, Maryland.

"Many, many years. Yes, sir," Wiget said. "I knew him when he was about 12 years old. He was one or two years under my tuition."[9]

In 1865, at Mary Surratt's trial, Wiget was asked about her character.

"It is about ten or eleven years since I became acquainted with Mrs. Mary E. Surratt," he said. "I knew her well and I have always heard everyone speak very highly of her character as a lady and as a Christian. During all this acquaintance, nothing has ever come to my knowledge respecting her character that would be called un-Christian."[10]

At institutions run by the Society of Jesus, residents traditionally keep a "house diary," a commonplace book chronicling daily activities – religious rites, the comings and goings of members of the community and visiting Jesuits. At the time of the Lincoln murder, the house diary at Gonzaga College seems not to have been kept, but the house diary for Feb. 4, 1863, notes that "A Mr. Sarrats who came here sick from the country about ten days since having recovered left this morning." Next to the entry is written "John Surrat."[11]

Father Bernardin Wiget was not merely a defender of fellow Catholic Mary Surratt but a forceful defender of Catholicism itself. His own faith was hard-fought.

A native of Switzerland, Wiget had been enrolled at the society's seminary in Fribourg when the government expelled all Jesuits. In disguise, he fled his homeland and, with many other Swiss Jesuits, was assigned to travel to the United States.[12]

He came first to Georgetown College, then to St. Thomas Manor, and later to Boston. There, he took on the city's Protestant establishment by organizing a sodality of Catholic boys some 800 strong and helping launch a social movement and a legal case known as the Eliot School Rebellion. Led by Wiget, Catholic students in public school refused to read Protestant versions of prayers or the Bible. Protestants attacked Wiget from their pulpits and in their publications.[13]

After Father Wiget left southern Maryland, St. Thomas Manor School foundered. When it closed in 1857, members of its student body, including Isaac and John Surratt, were offered the chance to

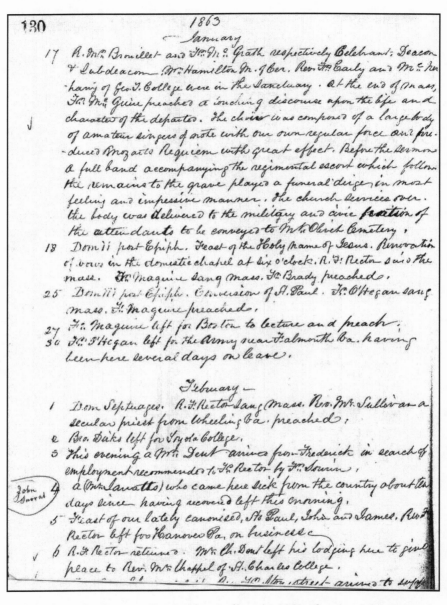

A page from the Gonzaga Jesuits' house diary in 1863, showing John Surratt's stay.

enroll at the College of Holy Cross in Worcester, Massachusetts, but the family couldn't afford it.[14]

Mary Surratt again took to asking clerics for help. In a letter to Fr. Wiget, she wrote, " ... As Mr. Surratt will not send Isaac to school and I have sent him as long as I have any means ... I hope Dear Father you will try and get him something to do as it will be so much better for him to be out of the sight of his pa ... "

Thanks to his mother's persistence, John was accepted at St. Charles Borromeo in Ellicott City, Maryland. When John enrolled in 1859, one of his classmates was Louis Weichmann, the former Gonzaga student who would become one of the prosecution's key witnesses.

Everyone at St. Charles admired John Surratt, Weichmann wrote much later in his *A True History of the Assassination of Abraham Lincoln and the Conspiracy of 1865*:

> He was tall, erect, slender and boyish with a prominent forehead and receding eyes. His nose was sharp, thin and aquiline; his face bore unusually keen and shrewd expression ...
>
> ... [John Surratt] was a very orderly student and one of the best young men I ever knew, and could not have been excelled by anyone. His reputation for conduct and deportment were most excellent.

In late 1850s America, slavery and secession were the main topics of discourse. The son of slaveholders, Surratt was a southern sympathizer, Weichmann knew. "But I do not recollect that he ever made himself offensive to another by the persistence of his views," he wrote.

Surratt and Weichmann left St. Charles Borromeo in July 1862. Surratt felt he had no priestly vocation. Weichmann wanted to be a priest but thought his progress toward that goal was being thwarted unfairly.[15]

Hoping to enroll at another seminary, Weichmann took a job as principal at St. Matthew's Institute (now St. John's High School) in January 1863. He had immense foreign language skills – he knew seven – and enjoyed reading.[16]

Weichmann's Gonzaga registration record from November 1849. Both his first and last names were spelled differently by the press and by him as an adult.

Soon after, Weichmann's former classmate, John Surratt, looked him up. Surratt's schoolboy look was gone.

"His appearance and manner had considerably changed since his departure from college," Weichmann wrote. "He was now more a man of the world, had a brusquer air, and was much more bronzed."[17]

Surratt's more worldly demeanor came from his new line of work. John was now a postmaster, operating the post office in his family's tavern and home in Surrattsville. His father had died in 1862. Since then John had assumed the role of proprietor at the tavern, a meeting place for southern spies and blockade runners.[18]

After reconnecting with Surratt, Weichmann traveled to Surrattsville to visit his friend's family. He received "a kind reception" from John, mother Mary, and sister Anna, according to his book on the assassination.

The day after Weichmann arrived on an 1863 visit to Surrattsville, he was awakened by music outside. Members of the U.S. Marine Corps Band had come from Washington to serenade newly-elected county officials.

"With them was a frowsy-headed youth of sallow complexion and coal-black hair who seemed to be a hail fellow well met among the whole party," Weichmann wrote. "Seeing me, he asked Surratt who I was. Surratt thereupon introduced him to me. His name was David E. Herold [1858]."[19]

The Marine Band no doubt was a welcome distraction for the Surratts. Mary Surratt's husband was in his grave and her eldest son, Isaac, was fighting on the Rebel side in Texas. The Civil War was at its height and fury.

John Jr. lost the postmaster job because of his suspected Confederate activities. More and more he was running Confederate dispatches north and south. He certainly wasn't making much of a contribution to the Surratt family's finances. So shortly after slavery was outlawed in Maryland in 1864 and the Surratt slaves were freed, the family began to make plans to move to Washington and run the boarding house John Sr. had bought some years before. By Oct. 1, 1864, Mary and daughter Anna were in the boarding house. A month later John Jr.'s friend, Louis Weichmann, became a boarder for $35 per month. Mary advertised for other boarders and had to

Assassin David Herold's Gonzaga registration page from April 1858.

Photo of David Herold that appeared on the reward poster after the assassination. Witness Weichmann said he helped obtain the picture from Herold's mother when he accompanied police to her house looking for him.

choose carefully from a city teeming with transients, scalawags and opportunists. Spies too easily plied their trade. One was Augustus Howell, who had spent considerable time at the Surratt tavern and now was visiting the boarding house. He befriended Weichmann and he showed the curious clerk how to use his Confederate cipher.[20]

In the wee hours of April 15, 1865, Detective John Clarvoe stood in the hall of Mary Surratt's H St. establishment, talking with her shocked boarders. He asked Mrs. Surratt if they could speak privately. He had some questions, he said. "Be very particular how you answer them for a great deal depends upon them," the detective told the landlady.

Clarvoe and Mrs. Surratt discussed the actor and supposed assassin, John Wilkes Booth. She said she last had seen Booth at about 2 p.m. on Good Friday. Once again, she told the detective she did not know the whereabouts of her son John, though she did say she had just received a letter he'd sent from Montreal.[21]

It was morning before the police left the Surratt house.

After breakfast, Weichmann and fellow boarder John Holohan went to the police station. Weichmann had in mind to tell all he had observed in recent months at the boarding house, events and patterns which in light of the Lincoln killing acquired new meaning. This was not the first time Weichmann had had misgivings about the household. Months before, at the War Department, he'd spoken of the motley Booth crew to fellow clerk D. H. Gleason. Now Weichmann planned to "answer truthfully every question put to me with an unblushing countenance and a sinless soul ... an upright manner never has anything to fear, and I knew that my life had been correct and honest."[22]

At the station house, at 488 10th St., Weichmann and Holohan met with Supt. Almarin Richards and detectives Clarvoe and James McDevitt. Weichmann described in detail the unusual goings-on that accompanied Booth's visits to the boarding house. He told of Surratt's suspicious behavior and that of Mrs. Surratt. He also described other characters in the drama: the German immigrant George Atzerodt, Lewis Powell, a muscular former Rebel who went by the alias Payne, and David Herold, the boyish pharmacist's helper.[23]

Hearing Weichmann's information, the police took him along on trips to southern Maryland and Baltimore, where they hoped he could identify the suspects. Prior to heading for Baltimore, the pious Weichmann attended an early Mass at St Patrick's with one of the detectives.[24]

But the conspirators' trail went cold, and the Washington detectives returned to the city, planning to look in Canada for Surratt, based on his mother's claim that he'd written to her from Montreal.[25]

Police work had led the authorities to focus on the Surratt boarding house. Louis Weichmann's statements intensified their suspicions, giving them no choice but to arrest everyone living at the Surratt house, even Weichmann, jailed in the Old Capitol prison when he returned from his latest foray with the police, a trip to Canada that failed to turn up John Surratt.

When fellow War Dept. clerk D. H. Gleason, who'd mustered out of the Union Army as a captain after being wounded, confirmed that Weichmann had in fact brought up odd doings at the Surratt household months before the assassination, Weichmann gained credibility with the police. Given to gossip and name-dropping, Weichmann at first had told Gleason of Booth's visits to the Surratt house as a way of gaining social cachet.[26] Then came March 17, 1865.

As Weichmann later told it to Capt. Gleason, John Wilkes Booth, John Surratt and Lewis Powell rode off that day with some of their crowd. They returned much later, quite distraught.

"After dinner, I returned to my room, and was amusing myself with Dickens' *Pickwick* when to my astonishment at about half past six [John] Surratt burst into the apartment," Weichmann wrote later. "I looked at him and he was much excited … He held a four-barreled Sharp's revolver in his hand: one that could be easily tucked in one's vest pocket … [H]e leveled his pistol at me and exclaimed: 'Weichmann, my prospects are gone; my hopes are blasted … '"[27]

Booth and Powell followed on Surratt's heels, whereupon the three went to Surratt's room. Convinced something was afoot, Weichmann went looking for Gleason. He didn't see the former Union soldier until the next day at work, where Weichmann confided that he suspected the group had been trying to run the Union

General Montgomery Meigs, brother-in-law of John Rodgers (1824), who secured with troops the Petersen House where Lincoln died and sat through the night with the President.

Huckleberry Cottage in southern Maryland, where Herold and Booth were helped by a Confederate spy after the assassination. It now sits on the property of the Jesuit Loyola on Potomac retreat house.

blockade, was attempting to engage in illegal cotton speculation or perhaps trying to escape to the Confederacy.

Gleason "told me to keep a watch on them and if anything occurred of a serious nature we would report at once to the Secretary of War," Weichmann wrote.[28] He said that afterwards little alarming struck him, but it would come out that Booth and his cohorts were upset that day for one reason: They had tried and failed to kidnap President Lincoln.

On March 17, the Booth gang had hidden along 7th St. (now Georgia Ave.) north of the city awaiting the President, said to be attending a play at a hospital there. But when Booth went to the facility, he found Lincoln was not to attend. Booth sent his men home. Several of them gathered with Surratt at the boardinghouse where Surratt lamented his fate to Weichmann. They all went to Surratt's room for privacy but Weichmann could hear sounds of great excitement and disappointment.

Booth's kidnapping plan was being pushed in order for the Union to readopt a prisoner trade policy. The Union had stopped exchanging with the Confederacy because there was a seemingly endless supply of bluecoats while the Confederates were down to boys and old men. Booth grandiosely envisioned his plan causing the South to win the war. He so craved the drama of it that he originally proposed snatching the President from his box at Ford's Theater and muscling the gangly and powerful President across the stage and spiriting him away through the back door. Even some of Booth's sycophantic co-conspirators knew that was ridiculous and told him so at one late night meeting at Gautier's restaurant.[29]

All through the conspirators' trials, their lawyers tried to paint Weichmann as a Copperhead, a Confederate sympathizer who perhaps had spied for the South but now was turning state's evidence because the government had bribed or threatened him.

Weichmann countered that he had gone to the police the day after the assassination, telling them he " ... knew of these men, (Powell), Herold and Booth, visiting Mrs. Surratt's; I stated also what I knew of John Surratt ... My object was to help the government."

Why did he do this, his interlocutor asked.

"My object was to assist the government," Weichmann said.

Had the government threatened or offered incentives for him to testify?

The Lincoln family's summer home at the Soldiers' Home. It was built in 1842 by banker George W. Riggs, whose son Elisha (1865) went to Gonzaga.

"Not at all," he said.

The deepest stain defense lawyers could smear on Weichmann was his relationship with known Confederate spy Augustus Howell.

Noting that Weichmann and Howell had been friendly, the defense claimed that Weichmann, who'd met Howell at the Surratt house, had offered to provide the secessionist spy with sensitive information on the number of Rebel prisoners in Union hands.

Not only had he not done so, Weichmann declared, but he had described Howell's activities to Capt. Gleason.

Then there was the very suspicious matter of Weichmann and a Rebel cipher. Howell had taught his new friend how to use the cipher, a means of rendering messages into and out of code, and even gave Weichmann the code. Weichmann, the language expert who was teaching himself the new skill of stenography, said he simply used the cipher Howell had provided to encrypt a Longfellow poem into code.

But if Weichmann wasn't in on the scheme, why had the plotters felt so free to talk of their conspiracy around him?

His explanation was that in his presence they only spoke of general matters and never about "their private business."

During the investigation and search for Booth, Weichmann remained confined in the old Capitol Prison, joining scores of potential witnesses, look-alikes, Copperheads, and other suspects. The war might have ended, but not the State of Emergency, and Secretary of War Edwin Stanton continued to operate under the suspension of the writ of habeas corpus that Lincoln himself had ordered in 1861.

The old prison recalled earlier hard times in the capital. It had been built in 1815, after the British torched the Capitol, to serve as a temporary home to the House and Senate. Private funds underwrote the construction.

After the Capitol proper was restored and Congress returned to it, the temporary Capitol had several lives, including service as a temporary home for the Jesuit college that Wiget now headed.

The school, originally known as the Washington Catholic Seminary, had opened in 1821, when Father William Mathews, pastor

The old Capitol Prison, once home of Gonzaga and later, the Lincoln conspirators. As a young Congressman, Lincoln lived in what would become its annex.

of St. Patrick's church in downtown Washington, persuaded the Jesuits at Georgetown College to open a seminary next door to St. Patrick's, even providing gratis the lots on F St. on which to build it. The school quickly attracted a non-seminarian student body, with boys as young as 8, even though it charged tuition. This broke the Jesuit tradition in Europe, but in the U.S. tuition was the only way a school could survive.

In 1827, the Jesuits in Rome, learning that the seminary was charging to educate boys, ordered the school closed. Incensed faculty member Rev. Jeremiah Kieley, S.J., simply moved the school to the old Capitol, calling it Washington City College.

As soon as Rome learned of the gambit, the Jesuits ejected Kieley from the Order. The school quickly failed, and the old Capitol became a boardinghouse along with the nearby Carroll Row, where a freshman congressman named Abraham Lincoln rented a room. When the Confederacy seceded, union officials commandeered the old hulk and its Carroll Annex as a prison. Perhaps its most famous inmate had been Washington socialite and spy, Rose O'Neal Greenhow.[30]

Greenhow had married her late husband in a ceremony performed by the former Gonzaga President, Father Mathews. Like many natives of the small city, she had a wide web of personal ties to the school. For instance, Greenhow was related by marriage to the Cutts family, senders of many sons to the Seminary and Gonzaga College, as it was renamed upon its Congressional Charter in 1858 after reopening a decade earlier. One of the Cutts girls, Adele, had wed Illinois Senator Stephen A. Douglas (Parent 1859), who lost to Lincoln in the 1860 election.

While Weichmann, his landlady, and the other suspects coped with vermin in the Old Capitol prison, John Wilkes Booth and accomplice Davey Herold were in southern Maryland, hiding in the woods.

After shooting Lincoln and galloping down F St., the actor raced pell-mell for the Navy Yard Bridge. He meant to get over it to southern Maryland, from which gang members planned to cross the Potomac River to Virginia.

Herold's task had been to hold the horses at Lafayette Square, near the home of Secretary of State William Seward. He was to

The Rev. William Mathews, second president of Gonzaga.

Southern spy Rose O'Neal Greenhow at old Capitol prison. Mrs. Greenhow had been married by Fr. Mathews and had a number of personal ties to Gonzaga.

Senator Stephen A. Douglas of Illinois, Lincoln's presidential opponent and father of two sons at Gonzaga.

serve as a lookout for Lewis Powell, whom Booth had assigned to enter Seward's home and kill him. Afterwards, Herold was to guide Powell to the rendezvous point in southern Maryland.

Powell pushed his way into the house, drew his knife and struck, but Seward's soldier-nurse and son fought back. Hearing the screams and shouts, Herold panicked. He rode off, leaving Powell desperate for a way to reach the rendezvous.

Herold had been among the first co-conspirators Booth enlisted in his plot. The two may have met first at T.S. Ward's apothecary in Washington. Booth, a seasoned reader of people, could see that the 22-year-old Herold was malleable and drawn to the actor's charisma. He felt Herold might be particularly useful, since Ward's drugstore was used by Secretary Seward.[31] Herold also had worked for William S. Thompson, Lincoln's pharmacist, in Thompson's store at 15th and Pa. Ave. Poisoning was one of the options said to have been considered by the conspirators, and where better to find poisons than at an apothecary? And to the actor Booth, what more dramatic end than one with a deadly potion.

Herold, born in 1842, had grown up near the Washington Navy Yard, between M St. SE and the Anacostia River. His family was middle-class, his father the chief clerk at the Navy store on the yard grounds. Herold lived among other families with ties to the Navy Yard and the nearby U.S. Marine Corps barracks. He was so enamored of the Navy and the Corps that his right arm bore an anchor-and-heart tattoo. Among the neighbors were the Sousas. Before John Phillip Sousa became the nation's most famous military bandleader, he supplemented his income teaching music at Gonzaga.

As an elementary school student at the Cox-Marlot School, Herold made an impression on schoolmate George W. Baird, who wrote in a letter of his days in grade school with Herold.

"In 1850, when I was seven ... the boy who sat next to me about my own age was David Herold," Baird wrote. "A little round headed, round eyed, round bodied boy whose general rotundity was completed by a voice that rolled his Rs. I envied David his disposition in that he got along with the big boys so well. When a big boy imposed on David, he would escape with a funny remark which was generally called witty, which generally got a laugh, and David was called popular."[32]

Herold went to Georgetown College, and on April 26th, 1858, enrolled at Gonzaga College, presumably after being asked to leave Georgetown.

In those days, Gonzaga's semester ended in July; the enrollment notes for September 1858 indicate Herold did not show up, his fate noted by the simple query, "Herold?"

Herold may have spent that fall hunting partridge with his father. The two sometimes would disappear for weeks on hunts in southern Maryland, even crossing into Virginia.[33] These experiences earned him extensive knowledge of the region's roads and woods -- knowledge invaluable to anyone needing to devise a plan to escape from Washington.

As a young man, the 5' 7" Herold often was mistaken for a boy, an error he did not correct by his behavior.

Dr. Francis S. Walsh (Parent 1855, 1863), a druggist, employed Herold as a clerk; Herold boarded with the Walsh family in their 8th St. house near the Navy Yard for 11 months.

At Herold's trial, Walsh testified in his former employee's defense that Herold was inoffensive and was "light and trifling in a great many things, more like a boy than a man. But I never found anything to find fault with in his moral character ... I considered him boyish in every respect."

So, too, did Herold's father, who stipulated in his will "under no circumstances shall the duty of settling my estate evolve upon my son David."[34]

Dr. Samuel McKim testified at Herold's trial that he never trusted Herold to deliver medicine to his patients for fear the feckless youth would tamper with the drugs as a prank.

Another witness for the defense, trying to cast Herold as a pawn of Booth, described Herold as " not endowed [...] with as much intellect as the generality of people possess."

After the trial, Weichmann offered his first impression of Herold in an interview with a noted journalist.[35] Herold, Weichmann said, was a "seedy, frowsy, monkey-faced boy."

Later, in his own book, Weichmann wrote, "How such an insignificant and puny character could have mustered courage enough to nerve himself for his terrible deeds to those who knew him best [...] is utterly incomprehensible."

David E. Herold.

Even co-conspirator Lewis Powell dismissed Herold, telling his captors, Herold was "a little blab. ... I was never satisfied with him myself and so expressed myself to Booth."[36]

During the conspirators' trial, all were demonized in the press, particularly in descriptions of their appearance. Newspapers of the day did not run photographs, so reporters of necessity sketched the defendants in words as the way to read into their actions and expressions evidence of guilt, stupidity or both.

So it went with Herold, characterized in coverage of the trial as "generally sprawled all over the platform, sometimes propping his feet on the rail, sometimes twisting around in his seat, but always grinning without comprehension. Occasionally, he would slide down on his knees and whisper between the rails to spectators seated near the prisoners' dock. The jailer would methodically advise him to get back into his chair. Herold generally obeyed without a word."[37]

Characterizations of Herold as childish extended to the circumstances of his capture. The son of the owner of the farm where he was caught noted that the suspect "was dragged away, whining and crying like a child, and securely bound to a tree in the yard ... He kept up his whimpering until the Captain had to order him gagged."[38]

Informed of his capital sentence after being convicted, Herold had called for his family pastor, Rev. Mark Olds, of Christ Church Episcopal Church. Herold's mother and six sisters were present as he waited for the minister to arrive. In the lull, they said later, David talked with another cleric, appearing indifferent to his own sentence of death.

Painted by his own lawyers as having limited capacity, Herold in his own alibi for accompanying Booth in his escape seemed to back up their assertions. Questioned after his capture, Herold said he was going to see a man about a horse.

The day of the assassination, Herold said, he'd gone south toward Piscataway, some 17 miles from Washington. He explained that he was hoping to sell a horse belonging to George Atzerodt, a fellow conspirator who had botched his assignment to kill Vice President Johnson. Instead, Herold went to Surrattsville and the tavern that had given the town its name. There he fortified himself.

Home of Secretary of State Seward on Lafayette Square. Herold and Powell attempted to kill him here. The home was built and occupied by the father of John Rodgers (1824).

Drawing of David Herold with his family the evening before his hanging.

"I believe I took one or two drinks," Herold said.

En route back to Washington, and feeling "tight," he said, he met Booth, who was headed the opposite way. The actor invited Herold to join him, the pharmacist's helper said.

"Come go back down the country," he said Booth had called out. "We will have a gay old time."

Herold said at first he balked, but Booth insisted, so he came along. The next day, Herold said, he heard "that Lincoln was shot by a man named Booth."

In later testimony, Herold said he declared to Booth "either you or your brother did it."

"No sir," Booth told Herold, according to Herold, "I have not done it."

Dr. John Frederick May (1826) treated Lincoln, probing the President's wound, and identified the body of John Wilkes Booth, from whom he had removed a growth.

find a large ugly looking scar, instead of a neat line. He said it corresponded exactly with my descrip.

Answer — I do recognize it, though it is very much altered since I saw Booth. It looks to me much older, and in appearance much more freckled than he was. I do not recollect that he was at all freckled. I have no doubt it

Answer. — From the scar, I think I could not be; but I also recognition in connection with the of the features, which though much changed and altered, still have the same appearance, I recognize the I think I cannot be mistaken. likeness. I have no doubt that it is the person from whom I took the tumor, and that it is the body of J. Wilkes Booth.

Jno Fred. May M.D.

Sworn & sub. td at Washington DC this 28 April 1865 before me, and

Dr. May's transcribed comments in identifying Booth's body.

Herold made to head off on his own, but Booth turned threatening, he said later.

"He told me he had murdered the President," Herold said.

The military tribunal convened to try the conspirators did not buy Herold's story, nor those of the others who stood to hang for the President's murder.

The officers of the court sentenced four suspects — Mary Surratt, Herold, Powell and Atzerodt — to die by hanging.

Samuel Mudd, Samuel Arnold, Michael O'Laughlen and Edman Spangler were sentenced to prison terms. Dr. Mudd, the country physician who set Booth's broken leg after the assassination, had met with him several times prior. Spangler was the stagehand at Ford's who briefly held Booth's horse during the assassination. Arnold and O'Laughlen were boyhood friends of Booth pulled into the kidnapping plot but who balked at murder.

The sentence given to Mary Surratt — the first federal hanging ordered for a woman in the U.S. — set off one of the most dramatic scenes in the assassination's wake.

Soon after Lincoln's murder, John P. Brophy, described as having taught at both Gonzaga and St. Aloysius school, went for a walk with Weichmann. According to Brophy, during their conversation, Weichmann made a shocking revelation, stating that he had lied about Mary Surratt to save his own neck. Brophy, who said Weichmann wanted to clear his conscience, claimed he insisted that Weichmann immediately write to Secretary Stanton to save Mrs. Surratt. Weichmann replied that it was too late because Stanton was an anti-Catholic and was determined to hang Mrs. Surratt, Brophy said later.

Brophy, who did not know Mary Surratt, took up her innocence as a cause. He went to the most influential newspapers with what he said was his new information but they refused to publish it. In desperation, he had a report on the conversation privately printed. Weichmann steadfastly denied saying anything like what Brophy claimed he had.

Even so, Brophy met with the prosecution and shortly before the conspirators were to hang he repeatedly went to the White House, trying to persuade President Andrew Johnson to grant Mrs. Surratt clemency.

Dr. Samuel Mudd.

With Anna Surratt, Mary's daughter, Brophy camped in the White House lobby, refusing to leave. Johnson refused to meet with them. And though the tribunal which convicted the defendants had recommended clemency for Mrs. Surratt, Johnson maintained to his dying day that he never saw such a recommendation.

As Brophy and a weeping Anna Surratt sat in the White House, Adele Douglas (Parent 1859), widow of Stephen Douglas and a St. Aloysius parishioner, came in. Mrs. Douglas, who also believed in Mary Surratt's innocence, had enough status to get a meeting with Johnson.

The senator's widow pressed the President, to no avail. No amount of pleading would change Johnson's mind, she told Brophy and Anna Surratt.

Hopes dashed, the two raced to the gallows to say goodbye to Mary Surratt. They arrived just in time. As Anna and Mary wept, Mary was led slowly to her waiting noose, flanked by two priests.

Father Wiget tried to comfort Mary Surratt with prayer as he read from his breviary. She clung to his crucifix to the last, when all save the conspirators, bound and shackled, backed away. At the order, timbers supporting the hinged floor were pulled away. Mary Surratt, David Herold and the others dropped to their deaths.

The *Washington Star*, owned by William Wallach (1824), reported thus on the hangings: "The last act of the tragedy of the 19th Century is ended, and the curtain dropped forever upon the lives of its actors, Payne [Powell], Herold, Atzerodt and Mrs. Surratt have paid the penalty of their awful crime."

Controversy over Weichmann's alleged perjury lasted throughout the century, with Brophy's allegations popping up now and again and Weichmann vehemently denying them.

Brophy, who married a grand-niece of President Tyler, moved to New York City, where he headed St. Louis College there and later worked in the court system.

While in New York, Brophy came out in support of Winfield S. Hancock, who as a Union army general had served on the assassination tribunal and who in 1880 was seeking the Democratic nomination for the presidency. Hancock's rivals attacked him for being one of those who killed an innocent Mary Surratt. Brophy wrote to the party convention that Hancock had favored clemency and urged that the blame be laid on civilian leadership.

Adele Cutts Douglas, widow of Stephen Douglas, who sought clemency for Mary Surratt.

*General James A. Hardie, assistant secretary of War and father of two
Gonzaga sons. Hardie served as intermediary between the government
and Mary Surratt's confessors.*

(Hancock won the nomination but lost to Republican James Garfield, who served only briefly before being shot, the nation's second assassinated president. Gunman Charles Guiteau was prosecuted by Richard T. Merrick, brother of William Merrick (1824). Dr. Noble Young (1822) was the physician at the prison where Guiteau was held. Young wrote that he believed Guiteau was sane, opposing a widely held belief.)

For years afterward, Louis Weichmann, who also was harassed for his role in the assassination's aftermath, worked at the U.S. Customs House in Philadelphia, a position he perceived as a reward for helping to convict the assassins.

Losing his job in a change of patronage, Weichmann moved to Anderson, Indiana, a small town where his brother, Fred (1850), a Catholic priest, lived. Weichmann opened a business school there. But hostility followed him even there; he was shot at twice.[39] He devoted considerable time to answering allegations against him, especially by Catholics who savaged him for betraying a fine woman of their faith. These attacks led Weichmann to spurn Catholicism. On his deathbed, Weichmann signed a statement swearing that he had told the truth about the assassins.

Catholics were not being hypersensitive on the matter of the Lincoln assassination. The murder, occurring as American anti-Catholicism was running strong, triggered charges of a Papist plot, with all participants incorrectly identified as Catholics when in reality only Mary and John Surratt and Dr. Mudd were of the faith. These mutterings didn't fade when it came to light that while hiding in Canada John Surratt had had the assistance of a pair of priests, or that he later showed up in Rome as a member of the Papal Zouaves, the Pope's army.

One Catholic who paid close attention to the case in more modern times was the Rev. Msgr. Edward P. McAdams of St. Joseph's Church on Capitol Hill.[40]

Father McAdams, who had known Father Wiget, told a researcher that the Lincoln kidnapping plot Louis Weichmann had described was well known in Washington before Good Friday.

"Everyone knew about it," he said, including Wiget, according to the priest.[41]

Richard T. Merrick, brother of William Merrick (1824), who helped defend John Surratt at his separate conspiracy trial.

John Surratt in Papal Zouave uniform.

But how did Wiget know about it? Was it simply wartime gossip? Or had the extremely religious and scrupulous Mary Surratt told Wiget of the plot in the confessional? A woman who throughout her life had leaned so heavily on clergy would likely seek to know the fate of her soul were she embroiled in such a plot. And how would the Jesuit have replied?

What we do know is that the day after the assassination, Wiget likely went to Mrs. Surratt's house. When detectives interviewed Mrs. Surratt after the assassination, she declared that on Saturday, April 15, 1865, she met with an unnamed priest. Later in the interview, according to its transcript, she repeatedly referred to a "Mr. Wicket." In hindsight, it seems highly likely that "Wicket" is a misspelling of the Germanic name "Wiget," since nowhere else in all the testimony or literature on the subject of the assassination does a "Mr. Wicket" make an appearance. Indeed, the 1870 census enumerator himself hears the Germanic pronunciation and misspells Wiget as "Wicket." In other words, Mary Surratt is telling the police she met Father Wiget the day after the assassination in a time of her dire need, though perhaps to help his institution and Church as well.

Some time prior to the assassination, someone at Gonzaga had loaned Mrs. Surratt a wheelbarrow. Gonzaga's most vivid and graphic connection to the Lincoln assassination is that simple wooden barrow. On its side had been painted a single word: GONZAGA. It's unknown why or when it was loaned but it was on Mrs. Surratt's boarding house property the day after the shooting. And Wiget wanted it elsewhere. An understandably nervous Wiget, according to McAdams, had the wheelbarrow removed even though Secretary of War Stanton had ordered the house and vicinity left alone. Clearly Wiget wanted to avoid any perception that there was any Gonzaga connection to the crime.[42]

The wheelbarrow story, ever more amplified and garbled, was handed down as oral history among Gonzaga students until well into the 20th Century. Washington, D.C., Superior Court Judge John Bayly (1962) recalls in his day fellow students talking about a Gonzaga wagon being at the Surratt boarding house and panicked Gonzaga administrators scurrying to retrieve it after the assassination.

Weichmann himself came to scorn Gonzaga and all who had anything to do with it or the Catholic Church. "The Catholics of

Washington have always persecuted me and they are at the bottom of this whole business," he wrote in a letter to an historian. "Brophy, Coyle [a journalist and Gonzaga parent] and Surratt are all bitter Rebels and they are all Catholics and Democrats. The first two have the advantage of being Irishmen and the meanest element in our politics is the Irish Catholic element. Brophy taught for Wigget [sic] a number of years and I can tell you in confidence that there were no two meaner Rebels in Washington in 1865 than Wigget and [St. Patrick's Pastor] Walters."

In 1886, Charles Chiniquy, a former priest, attempted to prove in his book, *Fifty Years in the Church of Rome*, that there had been a Vatican conspiracy to kill Lincoln.[43]

Chiniquy had a personal connection to the slain President. In his days as a lawyer, Lincoln successfully represented Chiniquy in Illinois in a dispute between the cleric and his bishop. Chiniquy, who subsequently left the Church, said he maintained a friendship with Lincoln for years, visiting him in Washington and warning him then that the Church was out to get him because of that case in Illinois.

In his book, Chiniquy quoted Lincoln as saying, "Without the sinister influence of the Jesuits, this war would never have been possible ... We owe it to Popery that we now see our land reddened in the blood of her noblest sons."

No independent sources show Lincoln to have had such views. Lincoln's son, Robert Todd Lincoln, whose brother-in-law went to Gonzaga, had a thought on those who attributed their views to his father. Said the younger Lincoln, his father's name was "a peg on which to hang many things."

Fr. Wiget witnessed the hangings of the convicted conspirators, and knew most everyone within the comparatively small Catholic community caught up in this, perhaps the most tragic development of the war. Yet not until 1880, and then only barely, did he leave any direct record of what he thought of the assassination. And that record is all the more puzzling since Wiget, as Mary Surratt's confessor, would have known the answer to a question he posed the day of the hangings.

In 1880, Wiget went to New York to witness Brophy's naturalization as a U.S. citizen. That afternoon a *New York Herald* reporter

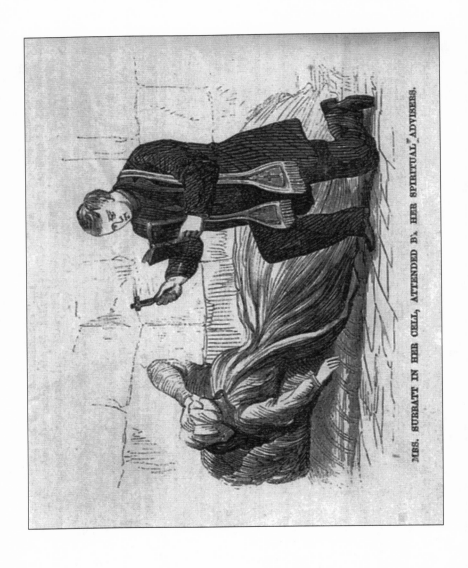

MRS. SURRATT IN HER CELL, ATTENDED BY HER SPIRITUAL ADVISERS.

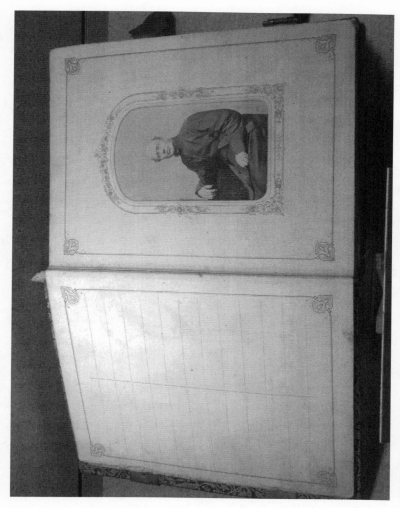

Bible of the Jenkins' family, with photo of Fr. Bernardin Wiget, S.J., Gonzaga president. Mary Surratt was born a Jenkins. Bible is at the Surratt Society Museum in Clinton, Maryland.

visited Brophy to ask his opinion on presidential aspirant Hancock's behavior toward Mary Surratt. He caught Wiget, who was about to race to catch a ship to Boston. The Jesuit defended Hancock, then told of a conversation he had had with conspirator Lewis Powell before the hangings.

According to the newspaperman's account, Wiget said he "embraced the favorable moment to ask [Powell] a question unheard by others. 'Laying my hand on his, so [...] I said in a quick, low tone, "Tell me, my friend, is Mrs. Surratt guilty?" Just as quick he answered, "No, she is not!"'"

Then, according to the article, Wiget described Powell "suddenly leaning forward and putting his lips to my ear he whispered: 'She might have known that something was going on, but she did not know what.'"

Further confusing the whole matter was Mary Surratt's request on the eve of her death that another specific priest come and attend her. That priest was Rev. Jacob Walter of St. Patrick's, whom, oddly, she barely knew. Walter contended for the rest of his life she was innocent and he had heard her last confession.

Why a woman about to die would choose a stranger for her final confession over a trusted family friend, Fr. Wiget, is a very tough question. And one posed in *Rome's Responsibility for the Assassination of Abraham Lincoln,* an anti-Catholic book by one of the trial's judges, Gen. Thomas Harris.

Harris contended that Wiget had granted forgiveness for Mrs. Surratt's real or perceived sins concerning Lincoln, then had Walter hear her final confession. Mrs. Surratt, now freed of any culpability in the eyes of heaven, could declare her innocence to Walter who could seek a commutation of sentence based on her declaration. Walter did seek to stop the execution and always contended she was innocent. Of course, Mary Surratt may simply have wished to cleanse her soul with multiple confessors. But did she know of the assassination plans or the abduction scheme? Convicted assassin George Atzerodt, within sight of the gallows and perhaps simply as a means to save a southern woman, declared her innocent, although he earlier in a police statement that came to light in 1977 implied she was involved at some level. Powell, too, declared her innocent as the gallows loomed, but told Wiget she did know something. Only

David Herold among those men hung that day seemed certain. Said Herold during his trial within earshot of defense counsel: "That old lady is in as deep as any of us."[44]

Notes

[1] Elizabeth Steger Trindal, *Mary Surratt, An American Tragedy* (Gretna, LA: Pelican Publishing, 1996), 42, and *Woodstock Letters* of Md. Jesuit Province, Vol. 12, p. 192.

[2] Jeffrey Wert, *The Sword of Lincoln: the Army of the Potomac* (New York: Simon and Schuster), 6.

[3] "Bernardine Wiget, S. J., and the St. Aloysius Civil War Hospital in Washington, D.C.", *Catholic Historical Review*, Vol. LXXVI: 4, 757.

[4] J. E. Buckingham, Sr., *Reminiscences and Souvenirs of the Assassination of Abraham Lincoln* (Washington, D.C.: Rufus Darby, 1894), 15.

[5] Michael W. Kauffman, *American Brutus: John Wilkes Booth and the Lincoln Conspiracies* (Westminster, MD: Heritage Books, 2005), 18.

[6] Paul Warren and Michael Dolan, *Echo Ever Proudly* (*Washington Star*, 1853, article reprinted), 41.

[7] Kauffman, *American Brutus*, 58.

[8] Trindal, *Mary Surratt*, 14. The account of Mary Surratt's early life and marriage are from this book.

[9] Burke McCarty, *Suppressed Truth About the Assassination of Abraham Lincoln* (Haverhill, MA: Arya Varta Publishing, 1973), 227.

[10] Benn Pitman, *Assassination of Abraham Lincoln and Trial of the Conspirators* Ed. Edward Steers Jr. (Lexington, KY: The University Press of Kentucky, 2003), 135.

[11] Gonzaga Archives.

[12] John T. McGreevy, *Catholicism and American Freedom: A History* (New York, W. W. Norton, 2001),19-20.

[13] Ibid, 8-9.

[14] Trindal, *Mary Surratt*, 45.

[15] Louis J. Weichmann, *A True History of the Assassination of Abraham Lincoln and of the Conspiracy of 1865* Ed. Floyd E. Risvold (New York: Random House, 1977), xiv.

[16] Ibid, xiv.

[17] Ibid, 18.

[18] William A. Tidwell, *Come Retribution: the Confederate Secret Service and the Assassination of Lincoln* (Jackson, MS: University Press of Mississippi, 1988), 409.

[19] Weichmann, *A True History*, 22.

[20] Ibid, 86.

[21] Kauffman, *American Brutus*, 58.

[22] Elizabeth D. Leonard, *Lincoln's Avengers: Justice, Revenge, and Reunion After the Civil War* (New York: W. W. Norton & Company, Inc., 2004), 99.

[23] Kauffman, *American Brutus*, 235.

[24] Weichmann, *A True History*, 219.

[25] Ibid, 220.

[26] Roy Z. Chamlee, Jr., *Lincoln's Assassins: A Complete Account of Their Capture, Trial and Punishment* (Jefferson, NC: McFarland and Co., 1990), 303.

[27] Weichmann, *A True History*, 101-102.

[28] Ibid, 109.

[29] Kauffman, *American Brutus*, 179-181.

[30] Chamlee, *Lincoln's Assassins*, 92.

[31] Ibid, 167.

[32] Burke McCarty, *The Suppressed Truth About the Assassination of President Lincoln* (Haverhill, MA: Arya Varta Publishing Company, 1924), 96.

[33] Buckingham, *Reminiscences and Souvenirs*, 31.

[34] "In Pursuit of ... Continuing Research in the Field of the Lincoln Assassination", published by the Surratt Society from newsletter articles (1976-1986), 24.

[35] *Surratt Courier*, IX-17.

[36] James L. Swanson, *Manhunt: the Twelve-Day Chase for Lincoln's Killer* (New York: HarperCollins Publishers, 2006), 336.

[37] Chamlee, *Lincoln's Assassins*, 318.

[38] Edward Steers, Jr., *Blood on the Moon: the Assassination of Abraham Lincoln* (Lexington, KY: The University Press of Kentucky, 2001), 203.

[39] Lloyd Lewis, *Myths After Lincoln* (New York: The Press of the Readers Club, 1941), 225.

[40] *Surratt Courier*, XI-29, article reprinted from *The Lincoln Herald*, (February, 1946).

[41] "In Pursuit of ... ", 287.

[42] *Surratt Courier*, VII-33.

[43] Charles Chiniquy, *Fifty Years in the Church of Rome* (New York: Fleming Revell Company), 730.

[44] Doster, William, *Lincoln and Episodes of the Civil War* (New York: G.P. Putnam's Sons), 277.

On the gallows. Mary Surratt is at far left sitting with Fr. Wiget on one side of her.

David Herold has the noose placed around his neck by the man in the white coat.

Lt. Edward P. Doherty led the cavalry troops who killed Booth and captured Herold. He married Catherine Gautier, sister of Peter (1852), and daughter of Charles, who owned a restaurant where the conspirators plotted to kidnap Lincoln.

Judge George P. Fisher, father of Charles (1864) and judge in the 1867 trial of John Surratt.

Joseph H. Bradley (1824), chief defense counsel for John Surratt in his trial. He had been asked to represent David Herold in 1865 but declined. Bradley and Judge Fisher fought so bitterly during the John Surratt trial that Fisher disbarred him, contending that Bradley had physically threatened him.

Robert Todd Lincoln, son of President Abraham Lincoln, and brother-in-law of William A. Harlan (1868).

Vice President Andrew Johnson is sworn as President in the parlor of the Kirkwood Hotel.

Fr. Jacob Walter, pastor of St. Patrick's Church, was called in by Mary Surratt to minister to her. Walter said he heard her last confession and said she was innocent.

Gonzaga President Bernardin Wiget led 250 of his students in the funeral parade for President Lincoln. They followed employees of the Washington Arsenal and preceded the Union Leagues of Washington, Georgetown and New York.

Peter Taltavull of the Star Saloon next to Ford's Theater and the man who poured John Wilkes Booth a shot of whiskey with a water chaser minutes before Booth went next door to shoot Lincoln. Taltavull was a musician in the Marine Band and grandfather of William Warren Taltavull (1906). Two other direct descendants are William Warren Taltavull III (1960) and George Kalas III (1990).

Appendix

Reprint of the Directory
of Gonzaga College students 1821-1882

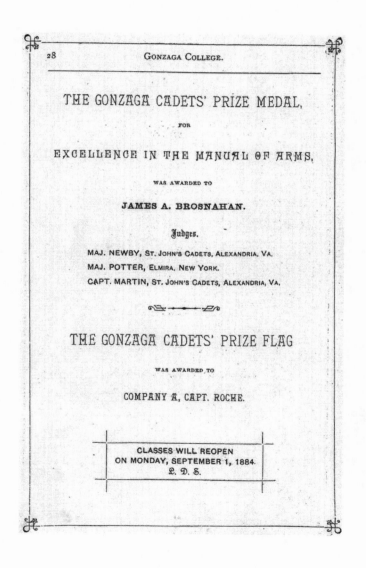

THE GONZAGA CADETS' PRIZE MEDAL,

FOR

EXCELLENCE IN THE MANUAL OF ARMS,

WAS AWARDED TO

JAMES A. BROSNAHAN.

Judges.

MAJ. NEWBY, ST. JOHN'S CADETS, ALEXANDRIA, VA.

MAJ. POTTER, ELMIRA, NEW YORK.

CAPT. MARTIN, ST. JOHN'S CADETS, ALEXANDRIA, VA.

THE GONZAGA CADETS' PRIZE FLAG

WAS AWARDED TO

COMPANY A, CAPT. ROCHE.

CLASSES WILL REOPEN
ON MONDAY, SEPTEMBER 1, 1884.
L. D. S.

When we published the list of students in June, 1883, we were aware of its incompleteness and were desirous of fuller information from those who could give it. We now feel satisfied with our experiment, and annex a fairly complete catalogue of former students of Gonzaga College, or of the old "Seminary." We trust that the names of the living here enrolled represent so many friendly patrons, who will be glad to aid us in upholding the fame of their Alma Mater by recommending new students to our care. Besides that, some may be able to give us a helping hand in the project we cherish of building a new college. The names given here run from 1821 to 1827, and from 1848 to 1859. The list given in the catalogue for 1883 includes the years from 1858 to 1882.

NAME.	YEAR.	OCCUPATION.	RESIDENCE.
*Anderson, G. Washington	1821		
*Arguilles, Louis	1822		
*Arguilles, James	1824		
*Allen, G. F.	1826		
Anderson, Joseph Dade	1848		
Anderson, Garrett	1848		
Anderson, W. H.	1849		
Allsworth, William	1849		
Ayres, Thos. B.	1849		
Ayres, Gideon H.	1849		
Astel, Richard V.	1851		
Anderson, James Marshall	1852		
Anderson, Charles	1852		
Anderson, John	1853		
Atkins, Joseph	1854	Clerk.	523 6th street n. w.
Alexander, Columbus	1855		1007 F street n. w.
Altemus, Thomas	1855	Engineer,	334 1st street n. e.
Adams, James Bradley	1855	Stationer,	803 L street n. w.
Adams, Milton G.	1855		
Alexander, Henry	1855	Stenographer,	1726 F street n. w.
Alexander, Walter O.	1855	Physician,	1728 F street n. w.
Anderson, George	1856		
Anderson, Thomas	1856		
Anderson, John	1856		
Blake, Joseph	1822		
*Boone, John F.	1821		
Brent, William	1824		
Bardston, Heli	1823		
Blanchard, R.	1824		
*Blanchard, Valentine	1824		
Brent, Thomas	1821		
Barry, Nicholas R.	1822		
Barry, Richard	1823		
Bartle, Samuel	1821		
Beall, George W.	1824		3260 O street n. w.
Baker, Lewis	1822		
Barclay, John	1823		
Brent, Henry	1823		
Barry, David	1823		
Brent, Robert Carroll	1824		
Barry, Robert	1822		
Brown, William	1822		
Baltzer, Robert	1829		
Barry, Edward	1822		
Berry, George	1824		
Barry, John	1822		
Balmam, Andrew	1824		

* Deceased.

30   GONZAGA COLLEGE.

NAME.	YEAR.	OCCUPATION.	RESIDENCE.
Banon, Peter	1824		
Bay, Mansfield	1823		
Berryman, Wm. Lerois	1822		
Berryman, Otway	1822		
Bradley, Joseph H.	1824	Lawyer,	Montgomery County, Md.
Bushey, Louis K.	1825		
Brooke, Edward	1825	Butcher,	Rockville Turnpike.
Burgess, Francis	1825		
Brent, J.	1825		
Bealle, C.	1825		
Burn, Henry	1826		
Bell, Phineas	1826		
Burk, James	1826		
Braerly, Joseph	1826		
Black, Samuel	1826		
Berry, William	1826		
*Boone, John Francis	1848		
Boone, Thos. B.	1848	Ag·nt Alex. & Fred'g R R.	Alexandria, Va.
Briscoe, Richard C.	1848		
Briscoe, Walter C.	1848	Physician,	317 C street n. w.
Burgevin, Henry	1848		
Brooks, Nicholas B.	1848		2500 P street n. w.
Butler, William	1848		
Barry, William	1848		
Butler, John	1848		
Butler, Henry	1848		
Brown. George	1848		
Brintnall, John P.	1848		
Burch, Vincent	1849		
Burch, George W.	1849		
Burch, William Henry	1849		
Beckert, Adolph	1849		
Bastianelli, Cajetan	1849		
Bastianelli, Ernest	1849		
Bastianelli, James	1849		
Berrit, Charles	1849		
Barrier, George	1849		
Beall, R. James	1849	Surveyor,	941 R. I. avenue n. w.
Brennan, John L.	1849		
Briscoe, Theodore	1849		
*Bulger, John	1849		
Boteler, Charles	1849		
Butler, John	1849		
Berryman, James N.	1849		
Blount, William R.	1849		
Berryman, William B.	1850		
Berryman, Edwin L.	1850		
Bowler, William W.	1850		
Bagnam, William	1850	Merchant,	523 13th street n. w.
Boyle, John Franklin	1850		
Bailly, William H. C.	1850		
Bailey, Charles B.	1850	Sec. Washington Gas Co.,	513 3d street n. w.
Bronaugh, Richard C.	1850		
Bowling, Robert	1850		
Brown, Robert	1850		
Barnaclo, Andrew	1850		
Barnaclo, William A.	1850		
Boone, William C.	1850	Physician,	Plainfield, N. J.
Brown, William Edward	1850		
Brown, Thomas I.	1850		
Brown, M. Joseph	1850		
Brown. Alexander	1850		
Boyle, John	1850		
Bright, Jacob	1850		
Bradford, Henry C.	1851		
Burch, Charles	1851		
Baker, Thomas	1851		
Baker, John	1851		
*Bibb, Henry	1851		
Bright, George S.	1851		
Beveridge, Benjamin F.	1851		
Bisson, William	1851		224 3d street n. w.
Bartlett, John	1851		
Burke, William	1851		

NAME.	YEAR.	OCCUPATION.	RESIDENCE.
Bell, William	1851		
Burch, John Thomas	1852	Lawyer,	721 8th street n. w
Burch, Henry C.	1852	Clerk,	2210 I street n. w.
Bulger, Vincent	1852		
Bulger, Raphael	1852		
*Bayliss, William C.	1852		
Brady, Michael	1852		
Burch, Wallace	1853		
Burch, N. K.	1853		
Burke, Michael	1853		
Brander, Lewis G.	1853		
Byrne, James	1853		
Byrne, Edward	1853		
Boiseau, John	1853		
Barry, William	1853		
Bayne, William	1853		
Berryman, John	1853		
Bronaugh, Thomas	1853		
Bronaugh, Lewis	1853		
Bronaugh, Augustus	1853		
Belt, William	1853		
Barber, Theodore	1853		
Barnes, William	1854		
Barnes, James	1854		
Bennett, John	1854	Clerk,	1443 Corcoran street n. w.
Blanchard, William	1854		
Burch, Thomas	1854		
Burch, John J.	1854		
Brashears, Joseph	1854		
Brashears, Adrian	1854		
Bayne, Robert	1854		
Beguin, Thomas	1854		
Ball, John I.	1854		
Birrane, Richard	1855		
Birrane, Thomas	1855		
Burr, Harrison	1855		
Burr, Henry	1855		
Brooke, Joseph	1855		
Becker, George	1855		
Barnes, William	1855		
Barnes, Joseph	1855		
Brand, Taylor	1855		
Brent, George	1855		
Brooks, Edw. Hamilton	1856		
Burke, Thomas	1856		
Biclaxi, Oscar	1856		
Biclaxi, Victor	1856		
Bateman, Henry A.	1856		
Bateman, James M.	1856		
Brooke, Albert	1857		
Burch, William H.	1857		
Boyle, Junius	1857		
Bateman, John	1857		
Bastianelli, Æmilio Tito	1857		
Bastianelli, Edward	1857		
*Beale, James S.	1857	Physician.	1123 14th street n. w.
Barber, Andrew	1857		
Birrane, Richard	1857		
Brooke, Edgar S.	1857		
Bateman, James	1857		
Bateman, Henry	1857		
Baxley, Wm. P. D.	1857		
Bromwell, Alfred H.	1858	Lawyer,	154 A street n. e.
Beale, Buchanan	1858		
Baxley, William	1858		
Baird, James W.	1859		
Baumgarten, Charles H.	1859		
Brosnan, Daniel	1859		
Brown, Charles	1859		
Clark, James	1821		
Cutts, Walter	1821		
Cutts, Thomas	1821		

32   GONZAGA COLLEGE.

NAME.	YEAR.	OCCUPATION.	RESIDENCE.
Callan, John	1822		
Cummins, Charles	1823		
Chauncey, Charles	1822		
Chauncey, Perter	1822		
Crossfield, William	1821		
Crossfield, James	1821		
Carr, Overton	1822		
Carr, William	1822		
Callan, Nicholas	1822	Notary,	1422 F street n. w.
Cummings, James	1821		
Coome, James G.	1823		
Crossfield, William	1824		
Crossfield, Joseph	1824		
Coyle, William H.	1822		
Crossen, Henry	1822		
Costigan, Francis	1825		
Costigan, John	1825		
Clark, William F.	1824	Clergyman, S. J.,	Loyola College, Balt. Md.
Carter, John	1824		
Carlisle, J. M.	1826		
Cartheny, Andrew	1826		
Cartheny, John F.	1826		
Callaghan, John	1826		
Caden, Joseph C.	1848		
Callan, James N.	1848	Lawyer,	1801 8th street n. w.
Callan. John F.	1848	Clerk,	108 8th street n. e.
Cox, John F.	1848		
Cox, Joseph	1848		
Carvallo, Charles	1848		
Cleary, Fr. De Sales	1848	Clerk, P. O. D ,	1229 13 street n. w.
Cleary, Reuben St. John	1848		Brazil.
*Clearey. William B.	1848	Clergyman, S. J.,	
*Cleary, Douglas	1848		
Cleary, James K.	1848	Merchant,	1517 35th street n. w.
*Causten, Manuel C.	1848		
Caton, George	1848		
Conroy, John	1848		
Conroy, Lawrence	1848		
Connelly, Daniel A.	1848		
*Carusi, Samuel	1848		
Collins John	1848		
Crane, Matthew	1848		
Coburn, John	1848		
*Chambers, Benjamin	1848		
*Carusi, Nathaniel	1848		
Carusi, Francis F.	1848		
Carusi, John M.	1848	Real Estate,	906 11th street n. w.
*Clare, William D.	1849		
Caton, Edward C.	1849		
Crosson, Jas. Fred'k.	1849		
Callen, George	1849		
Cassell, Thomas	1849		
Cassell Constantine A.	1849		
Cassell, George G.	1849		
Combe, Geo. Griswold	1849		
Cockrell, Samuel	1849		
Chripps, Charles	1849		
Caton, Emanuel B.	1849		
Coe, Benjamin E.	1849		
Carr, Edward A.	1849		
Carr, Thomas N.	1849		
Carr, Samuel M.	1849		
Caton, John	1849		
Cullen, Cicero	1849		
Cronin, Timothy	1849		
Cohen, James	1849		
Connor, John	1849		
Connor, James	1849		
Connor, William	1849		
Connington, John	1850		
Clarke, William	1850		
Cavanaugh, James	1850		
Cluskey, Michael	1850		

NAME.	YEAR.	OCCUPATION.	RESIDENCE.
Cull, James S.	1850		
Cleary, Thomas	1850		
Cullen, Ezekiel	1850		
Castro, Charles	1850		
Caho, William	1850		
Caho, John Thomas	1850		
Caton, John P.	1850		
Caton, Aloysius	1850		
Cleary, Emmet	1850		
Carleton, Frederick	1850		
Carvello, Washington	1850		
Cahill, Patrick	1850		
Calleghan, Francis	1850		
Coyle, John	1851		
Cavanaugh, Michael	1851		
Cavanaugh, Thomas	1851		
Catlett, Hanson B.	1851		
Calvert, Edward	1851		
Clarke, Clarence	1851	Civil Engineer,	501 Stanton Place, n. e.
Cooley, Algoma	1851		
Callan, Charles C.	1851		
Callan, Nicholas F.	1851		
Cumberland, George	1851		
Carney, John	1852		
Crutchett, Henry	1852		
Clare, George Gale	1852		
Conroy, Lawrence	1852		
Cleary, Robert Emmet	1852	Merchant,	Baltimore, Md.
Cronin, Martin	1852	Chief Eng. Fire Dept.,	404 H street n. w.
Clements, Lewis	1852	Dept. Col. Cus.	502 7th street n. w.
Callan, Charles B.	1858		
Codwise, Beverley R.	1859		
Cronin, Michael	1852		
Cullen, John	1853	Clerk, Pat. O.	469 Md. ave. s. w.
Cross, William	1853	Clerk Signal Office,	324 2d street s. e.
Cleary, Nicholas	1853		
Collins, William H.	1853		
Crutchett, Alexander	1853		
Crook, John	1853		
Clarke, Alpheus	1853		
Collins, John	1853		
Callan, Edward N.	1854		
Callan, Thomas H.	1854	Lawyer,	917 H street n. w.
Callan, Henry L.	1854		
Carrpll, William	1854		
Casas, Francisco	1854		
Cheever, Thomas	1854		
Coombs, George	1854		
Cox, Richard C.	1855		
Castell, George C.	1855	Engineer,	1437 Corcoran street n. w.
Callaghan, John	1855		
Coues, Elliot	1855		
Chapman, Wm. H.	1855	Ex. Pat. Att.,	736 12th street n w.
Combs, Wm. H.	1856	Merchant,	918 I street n. w.
Cassell, Wash Ignatius	1856		
Campbell, Charles	1856		
Combs, George	1856		
Corry, Henry C.	1856		
Corridan, James	1856		
Carroll, James P.	1856	Clerk,	711 Market Space, n. w.
Clark, James E.	1857	Building Supplies,	301 E street n. w.
Castleman, James T.	1857		
Castleman, Henry B.	1857		
Curtis, Charles W.	1858	Clerk, Pension Office,	409 A street n. e.
Dyer, Joseph F.	1821		
Dubousquet, Elzear	1821		
Davis, Charles	1822		
Drain, William	1822		
De Kraft, Frederick	1824		
De Kraft, William	1824		
Dyer, John T.	1822		
Deery, James	1823		

34   GONZAGA COLLEGE.

NAME.	YEAR.	OCCUPATION.	RESIDENCE.
Davidson, David William	1824		
Dunkinson, Robert	1824		
Dyer, Hannibal	1821		
Dwees, William	1822		
Dyer, Jordan T.	1822		
Diggs, John H.	1822		
Douglas, Wallack W.	1823		
Derry, James	1823		
Dyer, Giles	1824		
Dickens, Thomas William	1824		
Dickens, James Joseph	1824		
Diggs, Daniel	1825		
Diggs, George	1825		
Diggs, William	1825		
Duncan, Silas	1826		
Dyer, Thomas B.	1848	Merchant,	Richmond, Va.
Dobbyn, John Francis	1848	Claim Agent,	Pennsylvania.
Donnelly, Henry	1848		
Donevan, Joseph	1848		
Duvall, Hamilton S.	1848		
Dooley, James	1848		
Duvall, Robert	1848		
De Krafft, James	1849		
Dooley, John	1849		
Dooley, Michael Thomas	1849	Clerk Adj. Genl's Office,	221 E street n. w.
Dant, Joseph	1849		
Devlin, John J.	1849		
Devlin, James	1849	Clerk, Treasury,	1511 15th street n. w.
Dobbyn James	1849		
Dant, Charles W.	1849	Bur. Pntg.,	479 H street n. w.
Dubant, George	1849		
Donnelly, James W.	1849	General Land Office,	901 T street n. w.
Dowling, David	1849		
Dalton, William	1849		
Dowd, Dennis	1849		
Dawes, Charles	1850		303 N. Y. avenue n w.
Dawes, Samuel Taylor	1850		303 N. Y. avenue n. w.
Drury, Charles Walter	1850		923 N. H. avenue n. w.
Dyer, Austin	1850		
Dix, William A.	1850	Merchant,	1205 32d street n. w.
Donelan, W. L. I.	1851		
Dawson, John W.	1851		
Dowling, Fenelon D.	1851	Druggist,	316 4½ street n. w.
Donoho, George	1851		
De Vaughan, Charles	1850		
Drury, Joseph Sylvester	1851	Salesman,	923 N. H. avenue n. w.
Desmond, Cornelius	1851		
Drury, Joseph Thomas	1851		
Dawson, James Francis	1852	Clerk,	426 7th street s. w.
Daily, Robert Emmet	1852		
Dunnington, Charles	1852	Book-keeper,	106 C street s. e.
Dant, Joseph M.	1852		
Dawson, Joseph	1852		
Dooley, Francis X.	1852	Druggist,	301 Penna. avenue s. e.
Dundas, William O.	1852	Planter,	Abbeville, S. C.
Dooley, Silas	1852		
Doyle, Michael	1853		
Dyer, Joseph Tarbell	1853	Fire Insurance,	2256 13th street n. w.
Duvall, Benjamin H.	1853		131 Ind. avenue n. w.
Donn, Harrison	1854		
Drury, William C.	1854	Com. Merchant,	918 F street s. w.
Donoho, Lewis	1854		
Daly, Eugene	1854		
Duvall, Robert	1854		
Dyer, John	1854	Merchant,	Colorado.
De Vaughan, Charles	1854		
Dubant, Edward	1854		
Dubant, Mark	1854		
Deane, James	1855		
Donn, Oliver	1855	Agent,	517 R. I. avenue, n. w.
Donoho, John	1855		
Dall, R. McSherry	1855		
Dant, Charles	1855		

NAME.	YEAR.	OCCUPATION.	RESIDENCE.
Dougherty, Edward Dyer	1855		
Drew, James	1856		
Drew, Patrick	1856		
Douglas, Stephen	1856		
Drury, William L.	1836	Clerk, Census Office.	718 11th street n. w.
Dangerfield, R. I.	1857		
Dangerfield, Henry	1857		
Davis, Daniel	1857		
Donohoe, James	1857		
Donohoe, Daniel	1857		
Desmond, Cornelius	1858		
Douglas, Robert M.	1859		
Douglas, Stephen A.	1859		
Easton, David	1822		
Elliot, Jonathan	1825		
Edwards, William	1825		
Ennis, Philip	1848		
English, Morgan H.	1848		
Elwood, William	1848		
Elwood, Thomas	1848		
Eslin, Columbus	1848	Farmer,	Columbia Road.
Evans, George	1849		
Ewing, Charles Bernard	1849		
Ennis, William	1849		
Eslin, Charles E.	1850	Farmer,	Columbia Road.
Engle, Philip H.	1850		
Elliot, John	1851		
Easton, George	1852		
Easton, James	1852		
Edgar, William	1852		
Edgar, Robert S.	1852		
Eff, John	1854		
Eslerly, Frank	1855		
Ellicot, Henry	1856		
Entwisle, Thomas W.	1857		
Edwards, James T.	1857	Clerk Gen. Land Office,	1220 12th street n. w.
Fenwick, Edward	1821		
Franzoni, Amilia	1821		
Fenwick, Ignatius	1821		
Fenwick, Notley	1821		
Fleory, Augustus	1821		
Faest, Samuel	1822		
Forrest, Samuel	1822		
Francis, Edward L.	1822		
Fleury, Lewis	1823		
Flannigan. George	1823		
Ford, Joseph	1823		
Fitzgerald, Edward	1824		
Fitzhugh, Alexander	1826		
Fitzhugh, Percy	1826		
French, George Hordgrove	1826		
Ford, Alexander	1848		
Ford, S. C.	1848	Inspector Gas and Meters,	1309 10th street n. w.
Flemming, John	1848		
Fitzgerald, Eugene	1848		
Fitzgerald, Willard	1848		
Fitzgerald, John E.	1848		
Foy, Robert	1848		
Franklin, John P.	1848		311 C street n. w.
Flannigan, Mitchell	1848		
Fendall, Philip R.	1848		
Fenis, Philip	1848		
Fitzpatrick, Peter Paul	1848	Clergyman, S. J.,	Loyola College, Balt. Md.
Faharty, William	1848		
Fenwick, John F.	1848		
Fitzgerald, Robert	1848	Sec. Great Falls Ice Co.,	226 8th street s. w.
Fitzgerald, Joseph	1848		
Fletcher, Jaoles	1849		
Flemming, William	1849		
Fitzgerald, Serald	1849		
Fitzell, William Wich	1849		

NAME.	YEAR.	OCCUPATION.	RESIDENCE.
Fleury, Eugene L.	1849		
Fitzgerald, Thomas C,	1849		
Fletcher, Edward	1849		
Fitnam, Augustus J.	1849		
*Fitnam, Jerome	1849		
Fuller, Oliver	1849		
Fuller, Franklin	1849		
Franklin, Joseph	1849		
Franklin, Benjamin	1849		
Farrel, John	1850		
Fisher, James	1850		
Fendall, Willis	1850		
Fletcher, Joseph	1850		
Fendall, John	1850		
Farley, Joseph P.	1851		
Fitzgerald, Maurice	1851		
Fennall, Smith M.	1851		
Faulkner, George Ellis	1851		
Farley, Hugh	1851		
Forsyth, George William	1851		
Forsyth, James H.	1851	Clerk,	1207 9th street n. w.
Fitzpatrick, John C.	1852		
Foster, Jerome	1853		
Fitzgerald, Martin	1853		
Feeley, Dennis	1853		
Fendall, James	1854		
Fenwick, William	1855		
Fenwick, Ignatius C.	1855		
Fritz, Fred	1855		
Fenwick, George P.	1855	Physician.	504 6th street n. w.
Fennell, John	1855		
Fleishell, Francis	1855		
Fowler, James	1855		
Fennell, Charles	1856		
Fenan, Louis	1856		
Friebus, George Theodore	1857		
Friebus, Gustavus A.	1857	Architect,	2004 35th street n. w.
Foller, John	1857		
Faley, John	1857		
Foreman, J. Rosewell	1859		
Goldsborough, John R.	1821		
Goldsborough, Charles H.	1821		
Gallant, Edward	1823		
Gott, Richard	1823		
Goldsborough, Hugh Allen	1822		
Gardner, James	1823		
Green, William R.	1823		
Graham, R. B.	1822		
Graham, M.	1822		
Gilliss, James M.	1823		
Gray, William	1823		
Gahan, Nicholas	1824		
Granard, George	1824		
Gadsby, George	1824		
Goutheland, G.	1825		
Gideon, G.	1826		
Gordin, John	1826		
Graham, Richard	1826		
Gould, William	1848		
Greenleaf, Albert	1848		
Greer, Laughlin	1848		
Gainor, William Stephen	1848		
Galt, George S.	1849		
Galt, James M.	1849		
Galt, Lewis	1849		
Garner, William	1849		
Gordon, Thomas	1849		
Griffin, Michael	1850		
Grady, James	1850		
Gaddis, G. H.	1850		
Godwin, James	1850		
Gooch, William	1850		

NAME.	YEAR.	OCCUPATION.	RESIDENCE.
Gooch, Alban	1850		
Gray, Benjamin F.	1851		
Goldsborough, William	1851		
Grant, David	1852		
Gautier, Peter	1852		
Graniger, John	1853		
Graniger, Rudolph	1853		
Granger, Eugene	1853		
Glick, Henry	1853		
Glick, Lipmann	1853		
Grammar, Lewis	1854		
Grammar, William	1854		
Grady, Thomas	1854		
Gulager, Fred	1855		
Griffith, Selby	1855		
Greenleaf, Abner	1855		
Gorman, Edward	1855		
Gossler, Stephen B.	1856		
Guthrie, Benjamin	1856		
Guthrie, Julius	1856		
Gallagher, Francis	1856		
Gibling, Peter	1856		
Gray, Francis M.	1857		
Guthrie, John J.	1859		
Hurty, W.	1823		
Handy, Levin	1824		
Handy, Charles	1824		
Hoban, Joseph	1822		
Hall, Samuel	1823		
Harrison, Richard	1821		
Hoban, James	1821		
Hoban, Francis	1821		
Hughes, Joseph	1822		
Hickey, James	1822		
Hillman, Alexander	1822		
Hoban, Henry	1824		
Hamilton, William	1822		
Hamilton, John	1822		
Handy, Hevy	1824		
Handy, William	1824		
Handy, B.	1824		
Handy, E.	1824		
Hoover, Thomas	1824		
Hoover, Samuel	1824		
Hunt, William	1825		
Hurst, Uriah	1826		
Hill, Horkan	1826		
Heany, Hugh	1848		
Harvey, James H.	1848		
Harvey, Wm. M.	1848		
Harvey, Richard F.	1848	Undertaker,	921 7th street n. w.
Howle, Augustus W. Y.	1848		
Hoban, James	1848		
Handley, James	1848		
Hill, James	1848		
Houck, John Wm.	1848		
Home, John Washington	1849		
Hill, Augustine	1849		
Hill, William Francis	1849		
Hawke, Charles	1849		
Hagerty, David	1849		
*Holtzman, Marcellus	1849		
Holtzman, Francis N.	1849		
Higdon, Lewis Edward	1849		
Hagerty, Patrick	1849		
Howlett, John H.	1849	Builder	216 N. Y. avenue, n. w.
Howlett, Howard	1849		
Hurley, John William	1849		
Hillyard, Benj. Franklin	1849	Produce Merchant,	1825 7th street n. w.
Hilbus, James H.	1849		
Hickey, William Jos.	1849		
Howard, George L.	1849		
Harvey, George	1849		

38   GONZAGA COLLEGE.

NAME.	YEAR.	OCCUPATION.	RESIDENCE.
Harth, George	1849		
Helsetine, Charles W.	1849		
Houston, Jos. P.	1849		
Harbaugh, Daniel	1849		
Hicks, William	1849		
Howison, John W.	1850		
Howison, Henry L.	1850	Captain U. S. N.,	823 Vt. avenue, n. w
Hart, Francis	1850		
Hurdle, Alfred	1850		
Hurdle, Henry	1850		
Hurdle, William	1850		
Hellene, Clarence	1850		
Hellen, Walter	1850	Advertising,	1318 I street n. w.
Hirlely, Patrick	1850		
Howan, John	1850		
Howard, James	1850	Pension Office.	426 College street n. w.
Helfron, John	1850		
Hogem, John	1850		
Henning, Wm. H.	1850		
Henning, Marion	1850		
Hempler, Henry	1850		
Hoban, Lawrence	1850		
Hatch, Cowper Hat Spring	1850		
Hoffar, Daniel	1850		
Hurdle, Thomas	1850		
Hopper, John	1851		
Higgins, Edwin	1851		
Harrington, Francis H.	1851	Lieutenant Marines,	3407 N street n. w.
Harrington, Edward	1851	Clerk,	744 6th street n. w.
Harbaugh, George P.	1851		
Hurdle, Edmond	1851		
Horstkamp, William	1851	Builder,	809 M street n. w.
Holt, A. Jackson	1851		
Hollan, James	1851		
Hogan, Patrick	1851		
Hoover, John Thomas	1851		
Hile, Henry	1852		
Hicks, Wm. P.	1852		
Hill, James H.	1852		
Hill, Jos. L.	1852		
Hesslup, Lewis	1853		
Heckerson, John	1853		
Hellene, William	1853		
Hanna, John Francis	1853	Attorney-at-law,	505 D street n. w.
Happ, John	1854		
Hile, Henry	1854		
Hewitt, George	1855		
Hansel, George B.	1855	Clerk Sur. Gen'ls Office,	803 6th street n. w.
Hellen, Francis	1855		
Hollan, Thomas	1855		
Howard, John T.	1855		
Hurst, Thomas	1855		
Hurst, John	1855		
Hughes, William	1855		
Herbert, Joseph	1855		
Hook, Marcus R.	1855		
Hook, Oscar B.	1855		
Haels, Alexander	1855		
Haels, William	1855		
Hunter, William	1856		
Hunter, Thomas	1856		
Holt, Henry	1856		
Hines, Samuel	1856		
Holtzman, Robert O.	1856	Real Estate,	92? N. Y. avenue, n. w.
Hopkins, Charles	1856		
Handley, Wm.	1856		
Hunter, H. Warring	1856		
Humrickhouse, Charles	1856		
Hoskins, Orlands	1856		
Hamersly, Lewis R.	1857		
Hagerty, Francis P.	1857		
Hunt, Franklin E.	1858		
Herald David E.	1858		

NAME.	YEAR.	OCCUPATION.	RESIDENCE.
Ironside, Benjamin	1825		
Ivey, Clement	1853		
Inch, Philip J.	1851	Chief Engineer U. S. N.,	114 C street s. e.
Irving, Martin	1853		
Irving, David	1853		
Inch, Richard	1855	Ass't Engineer Navy,	130 Md. avenue, n. e.
Iseman, Francis	1857		
Jameson, Charles	1822		
James, Charles	1823		
Johnson, William	1822		
Johnson, Thomas	1822		
Johncheney, Phillip	1824		
Jones, Walter	1825		
Johnson, Dixon	1848		
Johnson, James H.	1848		
Johns, John	1848		
Jesup, Charles E.	1848		
Jones, Isaac	1849		
Joice, John	1849		
Jamison, Baker A.	1849		
Jefferson, Ralph	1850	Clerk P. O. D.,	1118 11th street n. w.
Johnson, John	1850		
Johnson, William	1850		
Jones, Jos. S.	1851	Clerk Pension Office,	601 E street n. w.
Jones, Albert B.	1851	Clerk Pension Office,	604 9th street n. w.
Jones, Zephariah	1849	Contractor,	1104 9th street n. w.
Joyce, John	1853		
Jenkins, Thomas	1854		
Jones, George	1855		
Julian, Philip	1855		
Jones, Leon T.	1855	Teacher,	2117 K street n. w.
Jones, Richard	1855		
Johnson, Charles	1856		
Jones, John W.	1857		
King, Charles F.	1824		
Kerr, Thomas	1824		
Kerr, Edward A.	1823		
Kneller, George	1823		
Kneller, W.	1823		
Kane, Robert Edward	1824		
Kane, Franklin	1824		
Key, J. I.	1824		
King, Francis	1825		
*King, Thomas	1848		
King, John	1848		
Keller, Charles	1848		
Keliher, James	1848		
King, Samuel	1849		
King, Lowry	1849	Scholastic, S. J.,	
*King, Joseph	1849		
King, William	1849		
Kelly, Thomas	1849	Builder,	1136 19th street n. w.
Kurtz, Benjamin	1849	Merchant,	809 Q street n. w.
Keyworth, John	1849		
*Kirby, John	1849	Engineer,	827 6th street s. w.
Kirby, William	1849	Salesman,	2034 8th street n. w.
Keating, John M.	1849		
Knott, John	1849		
Keyworth, George	1849		
King, George	1849		
Kenan, William Augustus	1850	Lawyer,	908 M street n. w.
King, Charles	1850		
King, Joseph	1850		
Keating, James	1850		
Kahil, George	1850		
Kerr, Archibald	1850		
Keppler, George Henry	1850		
King, Charles K.	1850		
Kieckhoefer, Adolphus	1850		1518 28th street n. w.
King, George	1851	Lawyer,	803 9th street n. w.
Knowles, John	1851	Clerk Q. M. Gen'l's Office,	

40　　　　　　　　GONZAGA COLLEGE.

NAME.	YEAR.	OCCUPATION.	RESIDENCE.
King, Norval W.	1851	Clerk Adj. Gen'l's Office,	1007 H street n. w.
Keef, Joseph	1851		
Kealey, Daniel	1851		
Kavenaugh, Benjamin	1852		
Keady, Denis	1852		
Kingle, A.	1853		
Kinsley, Joseph	1853	Clerk,	401 1st street n. w.
Keef, Richard	1853		
Kennedy, Thomas	1854		
Kearn, John	1855		2010 E street, n. w.
Kaiser, Julius A.	1856		
Kent, William L.	1856	School of Music,	Irvin street n. w.
King, Theodore I.	1856		
Kirk, Andrew William	1857		651 E street s. w.
King, Jacob T.	1857		
King, William A.	1857		
Kirkwood, Albert R.	1859		
Kirkwood, John H.	1859		
Lay, Albert	1850		
Lynch, Ambrose	1850		
Locke, Andrew	1850		
Little, John	1851		
Lewis, Francis	1851		
Lockery, John	1852		
Lockery, Charles	1852		
Lancaster, Samuel	1854		
Lee, Alfred	1855		
Lee, Alexander P.	1855		
Lee, Chapman	1855		
Larcombe, Thomas	1855		1817 H street n. w.
Lynch, Sevier	1855		
Lombard, Chas. W.	1855		
Lascelles, Francis	1856		
Lamb, Wm. B.	1856		
Lee, Arthur	1856		
Lee, Wm. H.	1856		
Lyons, Melville	1856		
Linkins, John F.	1857	Coal Merchant,	2444 F street n. w.
*Linkins, Lewis M.	1857		
Loranger, Philip B.	1857		
Lane, Lafayette	1858		
McWilliams, Joseph	1821		
Masi, Philip	1821	Music,	Norfolk, Va.
Millard, Edward	1821		
McLean, Charles	1823		
McWilliams, Leonard	1821		
Mattingly, John	1821		
Mathews, William Francis	1823		
Mathews, Charles H.	1823		
McWilliams, Albert	1821		
McCorkle, John	1822		
McCorkle, James	1822		
Middleton, William	1822		
Moore, Robert	1823		
Martin, George	1822		
Merrick, William M.	1824	Judge,	Maryland.
Miller, Thomas William	1823		
Miller, Lucius	1823		
Meigs, Francis Clark	1823		
Major, Daniel	1823		
McArdel, Henry	1823		
Moss, Charles	1822		
Morris, Charles W.	1823		
Moore, William	1823		
McDaniel, George	1823		
McDaniel, William	1823		
Middleton, James	1823		
Martin, James	1823		
MacDonald, George	1824		
MacDonald, William	1824		
Meitland, Alexander	1824		

NAME.	YEAR.	OCCUPATION.	RESIDENCE.
Meitland, Henry Taylor	1824		
MacDaniel, James	1824		
MacDaniel, Ezechiel	1824		
Medly, H.	1825		
McDonald, Otis	1825		
May, Frederick	1826		
May, George	1826		
May, William	1826	Physician;	2022 G street n. w.
May, Henry	1826		
MacCreery, Henry	1826		
McGruder, Thomas	1826		
*Mohun, Richard	1848		
Mohun, Phillip	1848		
Morris, Martin F.	1848	Lawyer,	717 12th street n. w.
Marron, John C.	1848		
Marron, Thomas	1848	Clerk,	104 6th street s.e.
Marron, James E.	1848		
Murphy, Charles M.	1848		
Murphy, Joseph V.	1848		
McCormick, William J.	1848		
Murray, William	1848		
Murray, Charles	1848		
Mattingly, John H.	1848	Clerk,	508 6th street s. w.
McCarthy, James	1848		
McColgan, John	1848		
McColgan, Charles	1848	Clerk,	1435 9th street n. w.
Maher, George	1848	Clerk,	1435 9th street n. w.
Maher, James	1848	Clerk, Capitol,	2106 Penna. avenue, n. w.
Morrice, Thaddeus	1848		
McCarthy, Charles	1848		
Moenster, William	1848		
McGuire, Frederick	1848		
McKenna, Andrew Patrick	1849		
Miller, James E.	1849	Merchant,	1312 13th street n. w.
Mullay, John C. K.	1849		
May, James Russell	1849		
Melcher, Charles Appleton	1848		
Mickum, George Gantt	1849		
McColgan, James	1849		
Murrey, George	1849		
McCarthy, John	1849		
Morrice, Isidore	1849		
Morrice, Marcellus	1849		2019 9th street n. w.
Mann, William S.	1849	Grainer,	1124 Park Place, n. e.
Marceron, Marcellus	1849		
Mohun, Francis B.	1849	Sec. Riggs Fire Ins. Co.,	1012 11th street n. w.
McGuire, Joseph	1849		
McKim, Josiah	1849		
McCarthy, Joseph	1849		
McCormick, Henry	1849		
McDuell, John L.	1849	Builder.	49 L street n. w.
Miller, William	1849		
Mayo, Robert	1849		
McDermott, Joseph	1849		1319 8th street n. w.
Marr, Arthur N.	1849		
Marr, James H.	1849	Insurance and Real Estate,	508 5th street n. w.
Mattingly, Joseph	1850		
McGill, John N.	1850	Clerk,	1808 H street n. w.
Martin, William I.	1850		
McCormick, Charles	1850		
Melcher, James	1850		
Marceron, Albert	1850		
Markland, Matthew	1850		
McGill, Charles F.	1850	Clerk Pension Office,	707 8th street n. w.
Moore, George	1850		
Moore, James	1850		
Morris, Charles A.	1850		
Morris, Thomas M.	1850		
McGill, George	1851		
Morton, H. Howard	1851		
Morton, William	1851		
Masi, William	1851		
McQuillan, Edward M.	1851		
Miller, John	1851		

42 GONZAGA COLLEGE.

NAME.	YEAR.	OCCUPATION.	RESIDENCE.
Mitchell, Landon C.	1851	Painter,	618 H street n. e.
Miller, John	1852		
McDonell, John	1852		
Miller, Philip	1852		
Mace, Edward	1852		
Murray, Samuel	1852		
Metcalfe, Theodore	1852		
Metcalfe, George	1852		
Marrow, James E.	1852		
McCormick, Henry	1852		
McCormick, Charles C.	1852	Clerk,	616 K street n. w.
McCormick, Lewis D.	1852		226 H street n. w.
Mahony, James	1852		
McNerhany, Frank	1853	Clerk Q. M. Gen'ls Office,	1107 F street n. w.
Marrow, William	1853		
Myer, Franklin	1853		
McCook	1853		
Melcher, William	1853		
McKenna, William	1853		
Mudd, Ignatius	1853	Merchant,	1514 Columbia street n. w.
Murphy, Thomas	1853	Clerk Treasury,	1225 L street n. w.
Molloy, George	1853		
Mosier, Theodore	1853		
Molony, Thomas	1853		
Moore, Frederick W.	1853		
McNamara, John	1854	Clerk,	811 G street s. w.
Muntz, Thomas	1854		
Muntz, John	1854		
McCarthy, John	1854		
McKinstrey, William	1854		
Mullen, John	1854		
Myer, William	1854		
Morgan, Charles	1854		
McElfresh, George	1855		
Marr, Samuel S.	1855	Clerk Gen. Land Office,	1415 10th street n. w.
McCauley, Henry C.	1855	Merchant,	220 B street s. e.
Murray, John T.	1855		
Masi, Frederick	1855		
Masi, Francis	1855		
McCarthy, Thomas	1855		
Moore, John T.	1855		
Mitchell, Benjamin	1856		
Mitchell, Robert	1856		
Meem, George	1856		
Meem, Cloriviere	1856		
Meem, Otto	1856		
Mitchell, Joseph	1856		
McPherson, William	1857		
Major, Duncan Kennedy	1857		
McNamee Charles	1857		
McCarthy, William	1857		
McCarthy, John B.	1857	Correspondent,	915 15th street n. w.
McNerhany, John F.	1857		
McNerhany, Edward Thos.	1857	Clerk,	1005 Md. avenue, s. w.
Nally, Denis	1822		
Noyes, George	1821		
Nondmenter, Eugene	1826		
Noyes, Joseph L.	1848		
Newton, James	1849		
Newton, Lewis	1849		
Norbeck, George	1849		921 D street n. w.
Noyes, Thomas	1849		12:7 N street n. w.
Nailor, Allison	1849	Livery Stable.	1100 I street n. w.
Newton, Walter	1849		
Noyes, George Henry	1850	Telegrapher.	2 I street n. e.
Noyes, Charles B.	1850		
Noyes, William F.	1850		
Noyes, James Columbus	1850	Clerk,	1418 Mass. avenue, n. w.
Nailor, Washington	1850	Livery Stable,	505 13th street n. w.
Newton, Albert	1851		
Noguere, John	1853		
Norbeck, William	1853		

NAME.	YEAR.	OCCUPATION.	RESIDENCE.
Niblo, Henry	1855		
Needham, Thomas	1855		
Nally, Charles F.	1857		
Neale, Francis D.	1859		
O'Neill, John	1824		
Orr, Pacificus	1825		
O'Callan, William	1825		
O'Donoghue, John	1848		
O'Donoghue, Florence	1848		
Orme, James W.	1848	Merchant,	1202 K street n. w.
O'Donnell, James D.	1848	Druggist,	751 8th street s. e.
O'Brien, John E.	1848	Book-keeper,	1127 4th street n. w
O'Brien, Samuel	1848	Prover,	933 New York ave. n. w.
Ousley, John	1848		
Ousley, William	1848		
Orme, George Theodore	1849		
Orme, Joseph P.	1849		
Orme, Francis	1849		
Offutt, Pezin	1850		
Offutt, Richard	1850		
O'Leary, Jeremiah	1850		
Ord, John S.	1851		
O'Donoghue, Patrick	1852		
O'Donoghue, Florence,	1852		
O'Dell, Thomas	1853		
O'Toole, Lawrence	1853		
Orme, Charles	1854		
O'Hara, George	1855		
Offutt, George W.	1855	Merchant.	3211 M street n. w.
Polk, Franklin	1823		
Pearson, Giles	1821		
Pierce, John Hardy	1824		
Pairo, Thomas	1824		
Pierre, John	1824		
Pierre, Hardy	1824		
Polk, Columbus	1824		
Pope, Frederick C.	1848		
Poletti, John A.	1848		
Perrie, Charles F.	1848		
Peetsch, Ham.	1849		
Peetsch, William	1849		
Peetsch, Charles	1849		
Phillips, Samuel L.	1849	Lawyer,	330 4½ street n. w.
Purdy, John	1849		
Pettit, William	1849		
Pettit, John	1849		
Pettit, Perry	1849		
Plant, Frederick	1850	Postal Clerk,	727 6th street n. w.
Plant, Andrew C.	1850		
Plant, Charles H.	1850		
Peters, Albert	1850		
Pettit, Henry	1850		
Pigges, William	1850		
Porter, William	1850		
Porter, M.	1850		
Plumber, James	1850		428 8th street s. e.
Padgett, George W.	1850		1111 7th street s. e.
Padgett, Robert T.	1850		
Purdin, John	1850		
Peters, Joseph Chrys.	1850		
Poor, John	1850		
Poor, William F.	1850		
Padgett, Francis M.	1851		
Purcell, Henry	1851		
Phipps, John	1852	Engineer,	1301 Union street s. w.
Perkins, Edward K.	1852		
Pope, William B.	1852	Physician,	
Plummer, William	1852		
Phipps, William	1852	Engraver,	505 11th street n. w,
Peters, George H.	1853	Lieutenant U. S. N.,	228 New Jersey ave. s. e.
Purbam, Lewis	1853		
Pilling, Frederick	1853		1356 15th street n. w.

44   GONZAGA COLLEGE.

NAME.	YEAR.	OCCUPATION.	RESIDENCE.
Perkins, Richard	1853		
Pilling, John W.	1853	Real Estate.	1301 Mass. ave. n. w.
Pilling, James C.	1853	Chief Clerk Geological Sur.	918 M street n. w.
Poole, Maurice	1853		
Pendergast, Patrick	1855		
Purdon, John	1855		
Purdon, Jos.	1855		
Plumer, William	1855		
Pollard, Edward P.	1857		
Peters, Arthur S.	1857		
Peters, Ignatius	1857		
Pritchard, Edward L.	1857		
Price, William C.	1857		
Peffer, Henry	1859		
Queen, Washington	1822		
Queen, John	1822		
Queen, Henry	1822		
Queen, Henry E.	1848		
Queen, Plunket	1849		
Quigley Michael	1849		
Rodgers, Frederick	1823		
Rodgers, Robert	1823		
Roach, Ferdinand	1822		
Rockendorff, William	1824		
Reddull, William	1826		
Rodgers, John	1826		
Ringgold, Walter	1848		
Ranahan, Francis	1848		
Ruppers, Anthony	1848		
Robbins, James	1848		
Ready, Morris	1848		
Roche, Francis N.	1848		
Reily, John Theodore	1848		
Roth, Andrew	1849		
Ragan, James	1849		
Reynolds, James C.	1849		
Reynolds, William C.	1849		
Reynolds, Alfred	1849		
Ratcliffe, Walter	1849		
Ratcliffe, James	1849		
Robertson, Edmund	1849		
Reily John	1850		
Ratcliffe, John	1850		
Ridgely, Henry	1851		
Rainey, Robert	1851		
Rainey, John D.	1851		
Rover, Thomas	1851	Merchant,	741 N. Capitol street.
Riordan, Rochefort	1851		
Robert, Jos. Edward	1852	Builder,	1129 24th street n. w.
Regan, James	1852		
Ronan, James	1852		
Richards, Francis	1853		
Richards John	1853		
Ryan, John	1853		
Ranahan, Bernard	1853		
Roach, William	1853		
Ready, Thomas	1853		
*Rover, John	1853	Priest, S. J.,	
Ready, Philip	1853		
Renshaw, James	1854		
Riley, Terence	1854		
Ridgway, E.	1855		
Robinson, John	1856		
Robinson, George	1856		
Redwood, William H.	1856		
Roach, Edward N.	1857		
Reynolds, Charles W.	1859		
Rudd, Royal S.	1850		
Suitor, Alexander	1823		
Selden, George	1823		

NAME.	YEAR.	OCCUPATION.	RESIDENCE.
Stewart, William	1824		
Scott, Thomas A.	1823		
Seaver, William	1822		
Sly, Benjamin	1822		
Steiner, Henry	1823		
Siousa, John	1823		
Smith, Franklin	1823		
Smith, Fleet	1822		
Sandford, Samuel	1823		
St. Andre, Durant	1824		
Sweeney, Hugh B.	1824		
Stettimius, George	1823		
Stettimius, William	1823		
Stelle, Thomas T.	1822		
Sullivan, George	1823		
Sullivan, James	1823		
Stone, Philip	1824		
Scott, Arthur T.	1823		
Sims, Francis	1824		
Sawyer, Joseph	1825		
Shekell, Francis M.	1848		
Shekell, Benjamin O.	1848		
Scott, George Francis	1848		
Smith, Leonidas	1848		
Smith, James	1848		
Stoops, Marcellus	1848		
Sweeney, William	1848		
Shafer, Charles F.	1848	Jeweler,	712 12th street n. w.
Shafer, Edward	1848		
Shafer, Francis B.	1848	Book-keeper,	712 12th street n. w.
Sanders, Reid	1848		
Sanders, Lewis	1848		
Smith, John E.	1849		
Scrivener, John E.	1849		
Scrivener, A.	1849		
Stevens, Eben	1849		
Sergeant, George A.	1849		
Savage, Samuel	1849		
Smith, Constant F.	1849		
Starbuck, Theodore	1849		
Sweeney, Edward Thomas	1849		
Steele, John H.	1849		
Scott, William Graham	1849		
Sherwood, James H.	1849		
Smith, Nathan A.	1849	Clerk P. O. Dept.,	616 E street n. w.
Scrivener, Thomas	1849	Clerk,	917 9th street n. w.
Southall, Tyler A.	1849		
Smoot, Joseph	1850		
Stuart, Frederick D.	1850		
Schad, George	1850		
Smith, John G.	1850	Book-keeper,	408 7th street s. w.
Smoot, Samuel	1850	Book-keeper,	1109 K street n. w.
Solers, William	1854		
Sullivan, John	1854		
Solers, James	1854		
Scott, Walter	1854	Clerk State Department,	2210 Penna. ave. n. w.
Stewart, James	1854		
Sweeny, George	1854		
Sears, Clinton	1854		
Sears, Julius C.	1854	Clerk,	805 Market Space n. w.
Slidell, Alfred	1854		
Sullivan, Thomas	1854		
Stallings, John	1854		1425 28th street n. w.
Sauer, Louis	1855		
Schwartze, Andrew	1855		
Smith, Philip	1855		
Sutton, John R.	1855	Harbor-master,	1411 E street n. w.
Seitz, William	1855	Merchant,	Bladensburg road.
Seitz, Agustus	1855	Merchant,	1238 I street n. w.
Shea, Nicholas	1855	Merchant,	214 13th street n. w.
Shea, John	1855	Clerk,	216 13th street s. w.
Shea, James	1855		
Sherry, Charles	1855		

46 . GONZAGA COLLEGE.

NAME.	YEAR.	OCCUPATION.	RESIDENCE.
Scott, Leander	1856		
Schall, E. I.	1856		
Schall, William H.	1856		
Smith, Francis	1856		
Stewart, Alfred	1857		
Smith, Thomas C.	1857	Physician,	1133 12th street n. w.
Stone, Samuel	1857		307 Va. ave. s. w.
Smith, Samuel W.	1857		
Semmes, James H.	1857		
Sioussas, John W.	1857		
Stephenson, Ambrose H.	1859	Coal Merchant,	1001 F street s. w.
Scott, Arthur	1850		
Stuart, Charles	1850	U. S. N.	331 11th street s. e.
Sanderson, William	1850		200 B street n. w.
Sharretts, Samuel F.	1850		
Sharretts, Grasin W.	1850		
Sioussa, Charles M.	1850	Tea Broker,	1811 G street n. w.
Stergeon. E. B.	1850		
Sweeny, William H.	1850		
Seitz, George	1850		1010 10th street n. w.
Seitz. John F.	1850		1009 N. Y. ave. n. w.
Sands, William Francis	1850		
Sands, Francis P.	1850	Lawyer,	1222 Conn ave. n. w.
Sands, James H.	1850	U. S. N.,	3303 O street n. w.
Semmes, John O.	1850		
Semmes, Christopher C.	1850		
Snyder, William Henry	1851		619 N. Y. ave. n. w.
Sauter, Henry	1851		
Sauter, Michael	1851	Confectioner,	1111 7th street n. w.
Smith, William	1851		
Semmes, William	1852		
St. Clair, James	1852		
St. Clair, Robert	1852		
Stewart, Charles E.	1852		
Smith, Samuel	1852		
Smith, William	1852		
Spencer, Davis	1853		
Solers. John	1853		
Simms, Jos.	1853		
Smith. John	1853		
Slye, Henry	1853		
Stewart, Thomas W.	1854		1007 E street n. w.
Stephenson, John F.,	1857	Express, B. & O.	913 F street s. w.
Smith, Charles E.	1857		
Smith, John M.	1857	Clerk War Department,	2916 N street n. w.
Selden, James C.	1858		
Scott, Channing M.	1859		
Sommers, John R.	1859		
Symms, Frederick	1859		
Towers, James M.	1824		
Towers, Daniel	1824		
Thorp, Franklin	1824		
Tyler, Benoni	1823		
Taylor, Alex. Meilland	1823		
Taylor, Henry	1823		
Taylor, John C.	1823		
Travis, E. L.	1826		
Tennison, I.	1826		
Tschiffely Albert	1826		
Tschiffely, Frederick	1826		
Tennison, William	1826		
Tayloe, Henry Augustine	1825		
Tayloe, Charles	1825		
Talbot, William G.	1826		
Thurston. John J.	1826		
Thomas. Charles W.	1848		1208 D street s. w.
Thomas, John M.	1848		3242 Grace street n. w.
Tewal, P. L.	1848		
Trook, John L. H.	1848		
Thompson, James V.	1848	Clerk, Patent Office,	923 9th street n. w.
Triplett. James	1848		369 L street s. w.
Tyler, Charles	1848	Teacher,	914 14th street n. w.
Tyler, W. S.	1848		

NAME.	YEAR.	OCCUPATION.	RESIDENCE.
Taylor, Richard	1848	Merchant,	904 7th street n. w.
Towers, Jos. Borrows	1848	Builder.	57 P street n. w.
Taylor, Jerome	1849		
Thompson, John	1849		
Taylor, Alexander Mc.	1849		
Taylor, William H.	1849	Physician,	619 M street n. w.
Towers, William H. H.	1849	Printer,	300 H street n. w.
Taylor, Francis	1849		
Talty, John	1849		509 6th street n. w.
Tucker, William E.	1849	Engineer,	409 C street s. e.
Tucker, Albert	1849		
Towers, James	1849	Clerk.	300 H street n. w.
Towers Chatham M	1849	P. O. Department,	1118 Park Place, n. e.
Thompson, Frederick	1849		
Thomas, James E.	1850	Clerk,	1210 D street s. w.
Thomas, Philip K.	1850		
Towles, Gilbert B.	1850	Patent Solicitor,	Brightwood.
Towles, Henry O.	1850	Merchant,	914 H street n. w.
Talty, James	1850	Plumber,	11 Grant Place, n. w.
Thorn, Owen	1850		1009 K street n. w.
Turton, George	1850	Contractor,	415 I street n. w.
Tretler, Charles	1850	Book-Binder,	
Toomey, John	1850		
Turpin, Henry W.	1851	Physician,	427 11th street n. w.
Triplett, Goldie	1851		
Triplett, Francis	1851		
Tilley, Bryson	1851	Lawyer,	413 4th street n. w.
Tuley, William Henry	1851		
Tuley, Charles E.	1851		
Thomas, Laurence	1851		
Thomas, Samuel	1851		
Thomas Joseph	1851		
Thompson, Jno. Meyers	1851		311 H street n. w.
Tucker, James H.	1851	Telephones,	807 8th street n. w.
Thyson, Herman George	1851	Clerk,	1339 15th street n. w.
Thyson, Thomas M.	1851	Merchant,	
Troop, Nathan L.	1851		
Troop, Samuel G.	1851		601 I street s. e.
Thorn, Thomas	1851	Merchant,	
Throckmorton, Charles B.	1851	U. S. A.	1212 F street n. w.
Talty, David	1851		1134 26th street n. w.
Tobin, James	1851	Granite,	908 N. Y. avenue, n. w.
Tyssowski, Joseph	1851	Gen. Land Office,	908 20th street n. w.
Thompson, Richard	1853	Merchant,	Spring Street Road.
Tingle, Amory K.	1853	Supervising Agt. Treas.,	
Templeman, George	1853		
Turner, James Henry	1853		
Towle, George	1853		
Tretler, Francis	1854		
Trenholm, John	1854		
Tree, Charles	1855		
Tyler, Stevenson S.	1855		
Tyler, L. Taylor	1855		
Trott, John	1856		
Taylor, Fairfax	1856		
Turpin, George E.	1856		
Turner, James H.	1857		
Tucker, Francis C.	1858		
Underwood, D. Moxley	1858		
Vinson, William	1823		
Veil, Edward M.	1823		
Vansent, George	1822		
Vanzenatt, George	1824		
Vinson, Charles F.	1825		
Visser, Julius	1848		
Vonderleher, Jacob	1848		
Venable, W. P.	1850		
Vedder, Joshua	1856		
Van Bussam, Andrew	1856		
Wharton, Charles F.	1824		

48   GONZAGA COLLEGE.

NAME.	YEAR.	OCCUPATION.	RESIDENCE.
Williams, Alexander	1821		
Walker, Daniel	1824		
Walters, John	1824		
Wright, William	1824		
Winn, William	1823		
Watkins, Christie	1821		
Watson, James	1821		
Warring, Joseph	1824		
Wimsatt, Joseph	1823		
Ward, James A.	1824	Priest, S. J.,	Loyola College, Balt., Md.
Washington, Samuel S.	1823		
Way, George	1823		
Warner, Alexander	1824		
Wirt, John L.	1822		
Wilson, John	1823		
Wallock, William D.	1822		
Waller, William	1824		
Wirtzs, William	1824		
Wadsworth, Denis	1823		
Wadsworth, George	1823		
Wells, Thomas C.	1823		
Warring, Basil H.	1823		
Wayne, William	1823		
Wells, James	1823		
Winn, William	1825		
Warner, Alexander	1826		
Ward, Caleb	1824		
Ward, John F.	1824		
Waterston, George	1824		
Wimsep, Joseph	1824		
Wood, Joseph	1825		
*Wallach, Richard H.	1824	Founder of the "Star."	
Watkins, Clarence	1826		
Watkins James	1826		
Washington, Richard	1848	Pay Insp., U. S. N.,	1604 K street n. w.
Wheeler, John	1848		
Willard, Stephen C.	1849		
Waters, William	1849		
Wiber, David E.	1849	Clerk.	1258 10th street n. w.
Wilson, Columbus	1849		
Williams, Charles	1849		
Willard, Caleb C.	1849	Proprietor Ebbitt House,	F, cor. 14th street n. w.
Wheatley, Francis	1849		3045 N street n. w.
Wilson, Calvin	1849		
Wilson, Russell D.	1849		
Weaver, William	1849		
Waters, John	1849		
Wiechmann, Lewis	1849		
Wiechmann, John	1849		
Ward, William	1849		
Wilson, Childs	1850		
Warring, Joseph	1850		
Weeden, John C.	1850		
Widdicombe. Henry	1850		
Willett, Joseph V.	1850		
Weirman, Eugene H.	1850		
Wiechman, Frederick	1850		
Wirt, William W.	1850		
Wilson, John Marshall	1850	U. S. A.,	1141 Conn. avenue, n w.
Wallingsford, Malcolm	1850		
Wilson, W. W.	1850		
Washington, Henry	1850		
Williams, William A.	1850		
Worthon, Charles	1850		
Williams, John Absolom	1850		
Wenig, Emile	1851		
Werden, William	1852		
Whelan, William	1852		
Werden, John Q.	1852		
Willis, Rodolph	1853		
Wise, James	1852	Clerk, Pension Office,	604 10th street n. w.
Waldron, John	1853		
Watkins, George	1853	Clerk, Pension Office,	1200 G street s. e.

NAME.	YEAR.	OCCUPATION.	RESIDENCE.
Watkins, Ludolph	1853		
Wilmarth, John J.	1854	Lawyer,	227 4½ street n. w.
Wheatley, George	1854		
Washington, John	1854		
Welch, James	1854		
Williams, James	1855		
Williams, William	1855		
Worthington, Henry	1855	Clerk, Pension Office,	426 11th street n. w.
Wimer, James B.	1855	Clerk,	1919 Vt. avenue, n. w.
Wells, Claudius	1855		
Walsh, John	1855		
Walsh, Francis	1855		
Wilson, John	1855		
Wilson, John	1855		
Weaver, Ashley	1856		
Walker, John	1856		
Woodward, L.	1856	Printer,	515 Mass. avenue, n. w.
Woodly, William H.	1856		Lincoln avenue.
Waggener, James M.	1857		
Waggener, Richard H.	1857		
Wilson, William	1857		
Waggeman, Francis	1857		
Weaver, James B.	1859		
Watterston, George	1857		
Watterston, Charles	1857		
Webster, Park	1857		
Webster, Clayton	1857	Gen. Pr. Office,	436 R. I. avenue, n. w.
Wimsatt, Samuel H.	1857	Lumber Merchant,	H st. near 9th, n. w.
Wigg, William H.	1857		
West, William B.	1859		
Wildman, James G.	1857		
Young, Noble	1822		
Young, Alfred	1874		
Young, McClintock	1848		
Young, Alexander M.	1848		1002 8th street n. w.
Young, Howard	1849		
Young, W. H.	1849		
Yates, Jackson	1853	Furniture,	488 Md. avenue, s. w.
Yates, Sandy	1853		
Yates, George	1853	Furniture,	506 8th street s. w.
Young, Albert	1855		

List of students who spent three, or more, years at Gonzaga College.

NAME.	YEAR.	OCCUPATION.	RESIDENCE.
Acker, Henry	1866		
Adamson, Alexander	1874	Clerk.	Boston, Mass.
Adamson, W. Eugene	1876	Clerk,	New York.
Alexander, Charles	1866		
Alexander, Frederick	1868	Merchant,	1525 Columbia street n. w.
Allen, Clarence B.	1866	Clerk, Int. Department,	1700 14th street n. w.
Allen, James	1871		
Anderson, Henry B.	1870		
Ardella, Lawrence	1866		
*Aylmer, Joseph S.	1863		
*Aylmer, Robert	1861		
Bailey, Charles F.	1862		
Bain, John F.	1879	Printer,	80 Defrees street n. w.
Bagnam, Albert W.	1861	Clerk,	523 13th street n. w.
Bagnam, Andrew J.	1864		
Bagnam, Peter L.	1861	Merchant,	523 13th street n. w.
Barbour, Harrison L.	1872	Law Student,	724 9th street n. w.
Barnaclo, William A.	1864		
Barrett, Timothy B.	1876	Professor, S. J.,	Boston College.
Barron, Alfred	1866	Builder,	806 K street n. w.
Barron, Otto	1867		
Barry, Francis J.	1881	Bureau Printing,	124 C street s. e.
Barry, John J.	1874		
Bart, Ambrose F. X.	1880	Clerk,	1253 8th street n. w.
Bastable, Walter D.	1870	Printer,	Cor. 8th & N streets n. w.
Bastable, John H.	1881	Printer,	1002 N street n. w.
Bastinnelli, Adrian	1868		

50   GONZAGA COLLEGE.

NAME.	YEAR.	OCCUPATION.	RESIDENCE.
Bates, George T.	1865	Lt., U. S. Marine Corps,	301 Delaware ave. n. e.
Bauer, Henry	1867	Teller, Met. Bank,	227 4½ street s. w.
Beal, Charles B.	1870	Clerk, Sup. Court,	927 F street n. w.
Bean, Francis D.	1868	Physician,	Hoosac Falls, N. Y.
Bean, John W.	1868	U. S. Navy,	517 8th street n. e.
Bechenbaugh, William O.	1864		Richmond, Va.
Becker, Edward	1865	Clerk, City Post Office,	203 F street n. w.
Becker, James B.	1865	Priest, S. J.,	Leonardtown, Md.
Benson, Henry	1868		
Bergling, George	1867	Merchant,	708 5th street n. w.
Bibb, Albert B.	1869	Topographer,	1300 L street n. w.
*Bielaski, Alexander	1867		
Biggins, Thomas P.	1871		
*Bischoff, Henry	1867		
Blanchard, Charles	1865	Clerk,	223 B street n. w.
Blanchard, Claude	1865		
Blanchard, Ignatius C.	1865		
Blunt, Henry	1869		
Blunt, Edmund C.	1869	Lawyer,	280 12th street s. w.
Boarman, Chas. V., A. M.,	1874	Physician,	1015 M street n. w.
Boarman, George C.	1871	Clerk,	1015 M street n. w.
Boarman, Wm. W., A. B.,	1868	Lawyer,	1015 M street n. w.
Bohn, Joseph A.	1865	Clerk,	344 Penn. ave n. w.
Boyle, John	1875	Journalist,	1454 Corcoran street n. w.
Boyle Watson	1874	Clerk,	1454 Corcoran street n. w.
Boyne, Henry J.	1871	Lawyer,	
Brady, John B.	1868	Architect,	493 E street s. w.
Brecht, Charles A.	1882	Builder,	44 H street n. w.
Bridgett, Bernard M.	1874	Clerk,	125 D street n. w.
*Bridgett, Joseph T.	1870		
Brigleb, C. T., Armin	1869	Lawyer,	Jersey City, N. J.
Brooks, William M.	1865		
Brosnan, William F.	1878	Clerk,	7 Myrtle street n. e.
Brosnahan, Timothy V.	1872	Professor, S. J.,	Georgetown College.
Brosnan, Aloysius P.	1875	Professor, S. J.,	Holy Cross, Worc'st'r, Mass.
Brown, Augustus R.	1868		911 D street n. w.
Brown, Hugh F.	1867		501 G street s. w.
Brown, Richard J.	1863		
Brown, William B.	1868	Clerk, Int., Revenue,	915 12th street n. w.
Buckley, Michael	1865		
Burch, Andrew A.	1807	Clerk,	714 5th street n. w.
Burch, Arthur	1867		
Burke, Michael J.	1861	Clerk,	1243 G street s e.
Burns, Edward	1867	Mdse. Broker,	633 G street n. w.
Burns, Francis H.	1867	Salesman,	635 G street n. w.
Burns, John E.	1874		
Burns, Michael T.	1874		
Burr, Charles E.	1870		
Burr, James G.	1878		
Byrne, James J.	1880		
Byrne, John J.	1882		
Cahill, Daniel	1865	Lawyer,	227 B street n. w.
*Caldwell, Charles M.	1867		
Caldwell, Joseph B.	1876	Musician,	1134 12th street n. w.
Callaghan, Daniel C.	1864	Lawyer,	712 D street s. w.
Callaghan, Edward D.	1870	Draughtsman,	1416 Columbian street n. w.
Callahan, Joshua B.	1881		
Carrier, George J.	1867		
Carroll, James W.	1868	Clerk, Post Office,	631½ S street n. w.
Carroll, John F.	1882		724 4th street n. w.
Carmody, Thomas J.	1879		
Chery, William L.	1864	Merchant,	2018½ H street n. w.
Chester, John A.	1871	Student, S. J.,	Woodstock College.
Chanier, Louis	1867		
Clagett, Howard C.	1873	Lawyer,	619 H street n. w.
Clagett, Maurice J.	1876		
Clark, Alexander S.	1872		
Clark, James E.	1863	Building Supplies,	301 E street n. w.
Clark, John Blake	1872		
Clark, Joseph A.	1880	Clerk, Adj. Genl's Office,	1437 S street n. w.
*Clarke, James H.	1864		
larkson, Francis B.	1873	Printer,	27 E street n. w.

NAME.	YEAR.	OCCUPATION.	RESIDENCE.
Cleary, Nicholas F.	1863	Lawyer,	Colorado.
Cleary, Robert E.	1861		
Clements, Albert F., A. M.,	1874		
Chilton, William B.	1870	U. S. C., & G. S. O.	225 Delaware av. n. w.
Clum, A. H. Waldo	1871	Druggist,	1530 12th street n. w.
Clum, Francis M.	1871		
Coburn, John M.	1871		
Colbert, James F.	1874		District Columbia.
Colbert, Michael J.	1880	Law Student,	631½ S street n. w.
Colclazer, Bernard J.	1882	Builder,	1845 L street n. w.
Collins, Denis	1864	Merchant.	412 New York av. n. w.
Columbus, Charles G.	1869	Postal Clerk,	741 1st street n. w.
Connell, Aloysius B.	1876	Clerk,	707 5th street s. e.
Connor, Valentine	1869		Baltimore, Maryland.
Conway, William A.	1881	Clerk,	
*Coombs, Michael	1867		
Cooney, Henry J.	1874		
Cooney, Richard T.	1876		
*Cooney, Thomas F.	1870		18 I street n. w.
Cooney, William P.	1875	Clerk,	27 G street n. w.
Costello, Robert F.	1879		
Cox, Albert W.	1865		
Cox, John T	1868		3316 N street n. w.
Cox, John F., A. B.,	1863	Lawyer,	3 Myrtle street n. e.
Cox, Samuel	1863		
Cox, William	1868		
Crampton, James C.	1867	Merchant,	
Crampton, John T.	1867		1307 H street n. w.
Cromwell, Stephen C.	1871	Journalist,	
Crow, Charles L.	1873		465 I street n. w.
Crowley, Benjamin L.	1865		
Crowley, William	1867		
Cuddy, John	1861		
Cullinane, John F.	1878		702 1st street n. e.
Cunningham, Matthew J.	1876		
Daly, John F.	1869		71 L street n. w.
Daly, Charles F.	1879		
Daly, John H.	1863		330 Missouri av n. w.
Davis, Daniel W.	1862		
Davis, John M. K.	1861	Lt. U. S. A.	609 6th street n. w.
Dennis, Walter L.	1868	Clerk, Sur. Genl's Office,	1410 N street n. w.
DeRonceray, Alfredo	1876	Artist,	22 E street n. w.
Dimarzo, John	1879		
Dingle, James B.	1864		
Donnelly, Michael A.	1865	Clerk, Treasury,	1923 I street n. w.
Donoho, George A.	1861		
Douglas, George A.	1870	Journalist,	1315 13th street n. w.
Douglas, Henry	1867	Clerk, A. G. O.,	1315 13th street n. w.
Douglas, William B.	1868	Clerk, A. G. O.,	609 6th street n. w.
Dowden, C. Percy	1879		718 3d street n w,
Downey, William F.	1881	Clerk,	713 L street n. w.
Downing, Charles W.	1872	Merchant,	1155 4th street n. e.
Downing, Mortimer J.	1880	Stenographer,	
Downing, Thomas R.	1867		
Downing, William H.	1869		415 K street n. w.
Doyle, Eugene A.	1882	Clerk,	
Doyle, John	1867		1618 5th street n. w.
Dunn, James M.	1869	Builder,	
Draper, William	1867	Builder,	936 E street n. w.
Drew, John W.	1871	Druggist,	707 M street n. w.
Drury, Charles S.	1871	Notary,	
Duffy, James	1865		1818 14th street n. w.
Dufour, Clarence R.	1864	Druggist,	1818 14th street n. w.
Dufour, Ringgold A.	1864	Clerk,	338 Indiana av. n. w.
Duhamel, William H.	1867	Lawyer,	
Dwyer, William	1865		
Einolf, Louis P.	1869	Engraver,	51 H street n. w.
Elbert, Balthasar	1870		St. Charles's Seminary.
Elbert, Caspar	1868	Theol. Student,	
Elbert, Melchior	1868		
Eliot, John L.	1867	Physician,	510 E street n. w.

GONZAGA COLLEGE.

52

NAME.	YEAR.	OCCUPATION.	RESIDENCE.
Eliot, Randolph L.	1867	Druggist,	1007 S street n. w.
Ellery, Albert S.	1868	Clerk,	1401 5th street n. w.
Elliott, Charles A.	1870	Lawyer,	222 N. Capitol street.
Elliott, James	1868	Clerk,	
*Elliott, John J.	1860		
Elliott. William	1865		
Emmert, Louis H.	1867	Builder,	318 12th street n. w.
Emrick, Henry	1867		
Ennis, Henry A.	1865		
Ennis, William	1865		
Entwisle, Thomas W.	1859		
Evans, John J.	1881		
Evard, John	1857		
Fainter, John J.	1881		110 G street n. w.
Fainter, William H.	1881	Printer,	110 G street n. w.
Fealy, Thomas	1865	Merchant,	1001 N. J. avenue n. w.
Fennell, Aloysius	1861	Printer,	610 10th street n. w.
Fennell, Francis P.	1878	Phonographer,	1021 2d street n. e.
*Fennell, John F.	1862		
Fenwick, Francis Y.	1867		
Fenwick, Thomas P.	1867	Merchant,	Ivy City.
Fishman, Milford	1868	Merchant,	627 I street n. w.
Fitzgerald, Edward A.	1865	Clerk,	214 4½ street s. w.
Fitzgerald, James V.	1864		
Fleishell, William L.	1882	Printer,	17 4th street n. e.
Flood, Samuel C.	1861		
Flynn, S. W.	1867	Tutor,	S. W. cor. 8th & K n. w.
Forney, Edward B.	1870	Lawyer,	
Frank, Jacob B.	1869	Merchant,	2120 Penn. av. n. w.
French, Eugene L.	1880	Student, S. J.,	Woodstock College.
Fugitt, Bradford	1865		
Fugitt, Francis	1865		
Fullerton, Francis De S.	1868	Priest, S. J.,	Jersey City, N. J.
Fullerton, James B.	1869		Chicago.
Fullerton, John Joseph	1869		
Gallaher, Edw. Marcellus	1871		
Garcia, Manuel J.	1871		
Gallant, Edwin	1865	Clerk,	1420 5th street n.w.
Galt, Frank	1864	Clerk,	339 C street n. w.
Garrett, Albert J.	1864		
Gedney, Charles De Forrest	1869	Coast & Geo. Sur. Office,	920 E. Capitol street.
Georgii, Maximillian W.	1869	Patent Office,	917 7th street n. w.
Getty, Alonzo	1867	Clerk, Adjt. Gen. Office,	823 18th street n. w.
Giesking, Henry	1867		
*Gleason, John	1866		
Glorius, Andrew G.	1869		317 R street n. w.
Glorius, George	1870	Florist,	317 R street n. w.
Glorius, Ignatius G.	1881	Clerk,	317 R street n. w.
Goddard, George J.	1864	Pension Office,	1135 8th street n. w.
Goddard, Henry G.	1874	Clerk,	920 New York av. n. w.
*Goddard, Vinton	1867	Capt. U. S. A.,	
Goodrich, Henry E.	1867		St. Mary's College, Md.
Gorlinski, William A. J.	1872		
Goswell, Douglass C.	1865		
Green, John M.	1870	Physician,	
Griffith, Fred. J.	1873	Private Secretary,	Relay Station, B. & O.
Griffith, James A.	1863	Clerk,	33 Mass. av. n. w.
Guild, Alexander J.	1871		
Hall, Baruch C.	1875	Clerk,	609 H street n. w.
Hall, Edward J.	1878	Printer,	630 K street n. e.
Hall, Henry W.	1863	Clerk, Pension Office,	421 New Jersey av. s. e.
Hallinan, James A.	1867		
Hamilton, Stanislaus M.	1873	Clerk, State Department,	225 Delaware av. n. c.
Handy, Charles W.	1867	Real Estate,	609 P street n. w.
Hanna, John F.	1858	Lawyer,	514 E street n. w.
Hannon, Eugene A.	1874	Theol. Student,	St. Mary's Seminary, Balto.
Hardie, Francis Hunter	1869	Lt., U. S. A.,	
Hardie, Joseph Cuyler	1869	Clerk, Q. M. G. O..	3004 P street n. w.
*Harlan, William A.	1868		
Harrison, Edward C.	1870		
Harrison, Patrick H.	1870		

NAME.	YEAR.	OCCUPATION.	RESIDENCE.
Harrover, William H.	1864	Merchant,	923 G street n. w.
Harvey, Benedict Fenwick	1871		
Harvey, James F.	1864	Clerk, Capitol.	913 E. Capitol street.
*Harvey, Thomas A.	1871		
Harvey, William A.	1867		
Hayes, Henry L.	1881	Student.	District of Columbia.
Healy, John P.	1878	Druggist,	207 F street n. w.
Healey, Thomas A.	1878		
Heiberger, Francis	1867		1901 Vermont av. n. w.
Hellen, Joseph A.	1871		
Hendricks, Martin J.	1879		
Henze, Henry	1870		
Herbert, Francis A.	1878	Clerk,	101 K street n. w.
Herbert, William A.	1864	U. S. C. & G. S, O.,	607 H street n. w.
Herlily, John T.	1873		
*Hilbus, George	1868		624 E street n. w.
Hickey, Edmund P.	1861	Clerk,	221 E. Capitol street.
Hickey, John F.	1861	Agent,	303 L street n. w.
Hickman, George A.	1869	P. O. Department,	Frederick, Md.
Hill, Owen A.	1880	Scholastic, S. J.,	409 H street n. w.
Hipkins, Clement C.	1869	Printer,	
Hoban, Lawrence	1860		625 S street n. w.
Hodgkins, John W.	1864		1307 9th street n. w.
Hodgkins, Joseph	1864	Druggist,	1315 10th street n. w.
Hoffa, Ancus M.	1860		
Hoffa, Noble S.	1861		Children's Hospital.
Hofer, Andrew F.	1876	Phar. Doctor,	814 8th street n. e.
Hollohan, Henry S.	1879	Builder,	Frederick, Md.
Hollohan, John S	1878	Scholastic, S. J.,	Boston College.
Hollohan, Martin J.	1876	Professor, S. J.,	920 New York av. n. w.
Holtzman, Robert O.	1860	Real Estate,	2812 M street n. w.
Hood, Charles	1867	Merchant,	719 19th street n. w.
Hood, William H.	1864	Bureau Printing,	920 R street n. w.
Holtzman, Ernest A.	1872	Clerk,	
Huber, Louis J.	1870		
Hudson, Thomas J.	1881	Clerk,	15 Mass. av. n. w.
Hurley, Daniel	1865		
Hurley, John	1864		205 12th street n. w.
Hurst, John	1861		207 12th street n. w.
Hurst, Thomas F.	1861		104 I street n. w.
Hussey, Bartholomew F.	1880	Clerk,	306 L street s. e.
Hutchingson Jacob L.	1881	Clerk,	306 L street s. e.
Hutchingson, William B.	1879		
Hyam, Victor	1867		
Hyde, George E.	1864		
Immich, Daniel B.	1871	Musician,	1137 8th street n. w.
Jack, Edwin	1864	Printer,	508 5th street s. e.
Jacques, William C.	1882	Clerk.	707 I street n. w.
Jefferson, Ralph	1860	Clerk, P. O. Department,	1118 11th street n. w.
Jewell, Walter	1864		
Jirdinstone, James F.	1870	Book-keeper,	1806 I street n. w.
Jirdinstone, William C.	1869	Draughtsman.	1806 I street n. w.
Johnson, Henry L. E	1876	Clerk, Post Office.	227 13th street s. w.
Johnson, William G.	1876		227 13th street s. w.
Johnson, Henry A.	1867	Clerk, Adjt. Gen. Office,	2459 P street n. w.
Jones, Albert B.	1860	Clerk, Pension Office,	604 9th street n. w.
Jones, Bennett S.	1882	Clerk,	1304 4th street n. w.
Jones, Francis	1868		
Jones, John	1866		
Jones, John W.	1863	Gov. Pr. Office,	404 E. Capitol street.
Jones, Richard L.	1860		1402 Pa. av. n. w.
Jones, Walter S.	1864		119 Pa. av. n. w.
Jones, William C.	1872		
Jones, Orlando A.	1870	Lawyer,	
Joyce, Andrew J.	1863	Clerk,	1124 11th street n. w
Joyce, George W.	1872	Carriages,	1124 11th street n. w.
Junghans, Daniel	1871		
Kaiser, John H.	1865	Draughtsman,	1742 F street n. w.
Kane, Denis	1865		
Kane, John	1864		

54 GONZAGA COLLEGE.

NAME.	YEAR.	OCCUPATION.	RESIDENCE.
Keady, Thomas J.	1882	Druggist,	609 2d street n. w.
*Kearns, John W.	1865		
Kearon, Robert E.	1867	Fourth Auditor's Office,	614 M street n. w.
Keating, George	1862		
Keefe, Henry A.	1868		
Keefer, Joseph J.	1869		
Keleher, Charles	1865		
Kennedy, Francis A.	1880		18 H street n. e.
Kerr, Denis M.	1876	Clerk, Pension Office,	491 Maryland av. s. w.
Kieckhoefer, Eugene	1868		
Kieckhoefer, Francis J.	1861	State Department,	1321 S street n. w.
King, Alexius S.	1870	Lawyer,	Denver, Colorado.
King, E. Hume	1868	Manufacturer,	1331 G street n. w.
King, George A.	1868	Lawyer,	1518 28th street n. w.
King, Henry	1861	Merchant,	814 7th street n. w.
*King, James B.	1865		
King, James H.	1861	Cashier,	1820 16th street n. w.
King, John M.	1867	Solicitor,	N. Cap. Cor. I street.
King, Theodore F. B.	1861	Clerk, P. O. Department.	3317 O street n. w.
King, William Bruce	1870	Lawyer,	908 M street n. w.
King, Zachary Taylor	1861		
Kirby, Michael J.	1878		
Kirkwood, Albert R.	1863		
Kirkwood, John H.	1863		
Klink, John C.	1867		
Kohlberg, Manfred	1868		
Kolipinski, Louis	1876	Physician,	400 K street n. w.
Krohr, John G.	1882	Clerk,	49 K street n. e.
			454 Mass. av. n. w.
Lackey, William A.	1875		
Lane, John I.	1880		
Little, Edwin J.	1874		
Lamb, William B.	1860		
Lawlor, Daniel M.	1873		California.
Lawlor, John H.	1868		
Lebois, Emile	1864	Clerk,	New York.
Le Compte, Simon B.	1859		
Leonard, George W.	1861		510 Maine av. s. w.
Lepley, William	1867	Agent,	1718 14th street n. w.
Lieberman, Charles D.	1862	Real Estate,	1435 L street n. w.
Larcombe, Thomas D.	1860		1817 H street n. w.
Littell, Joseph R.	1878	Patent Attorney,	1005 L street n. w.
Lloyd, Francis B.	1864	Gov. Printing Office,	814 3rd street n. w.
Lochboehler, George J.	1881	Phar. Doctor,	55 K street n. w.
Lockrey, Charles R.	1865		
Lynch, Millard F.	1871	Clerk, Pension Office,	128 E. Capitol street.
*Lyons, Thomas B.	1881		
Lucas, Eugene C.	1869	Pilot,	2151 Pa. av. n. w.
Lucas, Lorenzo A.	1870		2151 Penna. ave. n. w.
Magelhaens, Amadeus De	1871		Brazil.
Magruder, Geo. Lloyd, A. B.,	1868	Physician,	815 Vermont av. n. w.
*Magruder, James	1869		
Magruder, John H.	1867	Merchant,	1720 De Sales street n. w.
Maguire, Francis J.	1874		23 7th street s. e.
Maher, James D.	1869	Clerk, Capitol,	2106 Pa. av. n. w.
Mahorney, George B.	1865		
Malone, Edward J.	1880	Gov. Printing Office,	728 2d street n. e.
Marriett, Joseph	1868		
Mann, William S.	1866		2019 9th street n. w.
Marceron, Edward K. J.	1882		416 4th street s. e.
Marceron, Joseph L.	1866		
Marll, Francis de Sales	1868		927 9th street n. w.
Marr, James Donelan	1872	Clergyman,	Baltimore, Md.
Marr, John Marron	1869		
May, George J.	1873	Clerk,	Seventh street road n. w.
May, Ernest	1872		
McAnally, Thomas F.	1880		
McCaffrey, Hugh R.	1874	Printer,	807 I street n. w.
McCaffrey, James D.	1872		
McCaffrey, William H.	1874		
McCarthy, Christopher P.	1875		
McCarthy, Jeremiah J.	1878	Clerk,	201 Mass. av. n. w.

NAME.	YEAR.	OCCUPATION.	RESIDENCE.
McCarthy, John	1865		201 Mass. av. n. w.
McCarthy, John B.	1860	Journalist,	915 15th street n. w.
McCarthy, Thomas	1860		
McClosky, William R.	1869	Merchant,	1030 7th street n. w.
McCollum, Joseph A.	1873		59 K street n. e.
McDermott, Francis M.	1880	Bookkeeper,	313 Missouri av. n. w.
McDermott, John A.	1878	Student,	313 Missouri av. n. w.
McElfresh, Francis	1866		609 F street n. w.
McElfresh, John	1866	Builder,	609 F street n. w.
McGarraghy, James J.	1880		
*McGivern, Daniel H.	1873		
McGlenn, Thomas	1867		
McGrann, William H.	1875	Clerk,	208 B street n. w.
McGrath, James	1863	Merchant,	1600 32d street n. w.
McLeran, John A.	1879	Clerk,	631 Q street n. w.
McKiever, Clement M.	1868		907 21st street n. w.
McMahon, Michael P.	1879		
McManus, James	1864		
McManus, John J.	1864	Book-keeper,	1429 New York av. n. w.
*McNamee, Charles F.	1862		116 E. Capitol street.
McNamee, John	1866		116 E. Capitol street.
McNamee, Samuel S.	1867	Clerk,	
McNamee, William	1864		
McNerhany, Edward T.	1862	Clerk,	1005 Maryland av. s. w.
McNerhany, James A.	1873	Printer,	1005 Maryland av. s. w.
McNerhany, John F.	1862		
Melhorn, Henry C.	1865		629 Q street n. w.
Menke, George	1869	Merchant,	608 3d street n. w.
Menke, John	1872	Physician,	
*Menke, John	1872	Physician,	New York.
Merritt, William E. H.	1874	Clerk,	914 8th street s. e.
Miller, Edwin	1874	Printer,	451 G street n. w.
Mitchell, Patrick Henry	1874	Book-keeper,	523 6th street n.w.
Mohun, William Ward	1873	Lawyer,	
Moise, Aaron W.	1861		918 E street n. w.
Morgan, E. Carroll, A. M.	1874	Physician,	905 E street n. w.
Morgan, James D.	1875	Medical Student,	933 N. Jersey av. n. w.
Moreland, Walter M.	1867	Clerk,	
Mosher, James	1872	Physician,	1413 R. Island av. n. w.
Mudd, Aloysius J.	1860	Journalist,	
Mudd, Ernest	1867		1429 Ohio av. n. w.
Mulcahy, Michael	1868		142 F street n. e.
Mullan, Henry A.	1881	Clerk,	120 1st street n. w.
Mulcare, Maurice A.	1880		208 D street n. w.
Murray, Francis E.	1871		1536 16th street n. w.
Murray, Neal T.	1870	Lawyer,	1404 6th street n. w.
Murray, Samuel H.	1861	Clerk,	
Murray, Stanislas I.	1863		New York.
Murphy, Alfred H.	1874		
Murphy, Laurence	1865		
Myers, John H.	1864		1406 E street n. w.
Naylor, Notley	1865	Superintendent,	1406 E street n. w.
Naylor, William	1865	Draughtsman,	
*Nalley, Charles F.	1863	Physician,	
Nathan Augustus	1867		
Neale, Francis D.	1864	Clerk, S. G. Office,	615 7th street n. w.
Neale, Richard T.	1864	Physician,	808 9th street n. w.
Neumeyer, Edwin H.	1868	Merchant,	1219 G street n. w.
Nicholson, Augustus A.	1873	Insurance,	216 N. Jersey av. s. e.
Nicholson, Daniel Carroll	1866		
Nolan, Michael P.	1880	Bureau Printing,	92 Myrtle street n. e.
Noyes, Clarence	1868		
Noyes, John T.	1861		
Obold, Sebastian F.	1878		123 D street s. e.
Offutt, George W	1861	Merchant,	3211 M street n. w.
O'Brien, Michael P.	1880		
O'Connell, Jeremiah A.	1878		51 K street n. w.
O'Connor, James F.	1878	Printer,	Frederick, Md.
O'Connor, James J.	1880	Scholastic, S. J.,	1007 9th street n. w.
O'Connor, Jeremiah J.	1876	Stenographer,	
O'Connor, J. Vincent	1882		
O'Connor, John W.	1876		

56   GONZAGA COLLEGE.

NAME	YEAR	OCCUPATION.	RESIDENCE.
O'Connor, William H.	1876		
O'Connor, William P.	1880	Scholastic, S. J.,	Frederick Md.
O'Dowd, James	1868		
O'Dowd, Richard	1868	Clerk, A. G. O.,	2106 G street n. w.
O'Meara, John U.	1864	Merchant,	227 B street n. w.
O'Neil, James A.	1880	Clerk,	216 3d street n. e.
O'Rourke, James W.	1875	Printer,	720 6th street n. w.
Ostermeyer, George	1866		314 Virginia av. s. w.
Otterback, William Henry	1866		
Oulahan, John K.	1868	Clerk,	614 A street s. e.
O'Leary, Daniel	1868	Clerk,	
*O'Leary, Charles W.	1868	Physician,	
*O'Leary, Theodore	1868	Printer,	
O'Connor, Francis J.	1872		
Page, Edward Byrd	1865		
Parker, Charles G.	1868		1415 11th street n.w.
Parkinson, Charles W.	1861		
Parsons, John	1862	Physician,	8 I street n. e.
Pearson, Henry T.	1880		
Phelan, Ignatius	1868		
Phillips, John H.	1870		
Plant, Edward H.	1869		
Polkinhorn, Henry B.	1866	Stationer,	228 2d street n. w.
Poole, John B.	1864	Lawyer,	
Pope, William B.	1860	Clerk, Treasury,	1217 6th street n. w.
Poulton, Henry M.	1871		
Power, James	1867		
Prosise, John L.	1876	Clerk,	1365 C street s. w.
Quicksall, William F.	1860	Lawyer,	723 13th street n. w.
Quill, Patrick	1870	Student, S. J.,	Woodstock College, Md.
Ratcliffe, Joseph	1864		
Randolph, Thomas	1871		
Reiss, William E.	1865		
Reiss, Benjamin	1865	Music,	
Renner, William D.	1868		
Repetti, George R.	1867	Merchant,	1308 3d street s. e.
Repetti, Joseph A.	1869	Merchant,	1610 14th street n. w.
Reynolds, William B.	1875		
Rice, Edward	1868		
Richards, Thomas	1867		
Richards, William H.	1867	Clerk, Treasury,	810 M street n. w.
Ricketts, William	1866	Clerk,	933 H street n. w.
Riggs, Edward F.	1875		611 H street n. w.
Riggs, Francis E.	1867	Banker,	1447 Mass av. n. w.
Riggs, John T.	1875		
Riggs, Thomas L.	1874	Banker,	1617 I street n. w.
Riley, John F.	1862	Lawyer,	315 Missouri av. n. w.
Riordan, John A.	1869		
Riordan, Rochford B.	1869	Editor,	Charleston, S. C.
Roach, Henry C N.	1860		
Roach, Joseph Edward	1870		
Robbins, William Drayton	1864		
Robertson, James P.	1871		207 3d street s. e.
Robinson, George	1871		
Rosenbaum, David	1865		
Roth, Benedict	1860	Manufacturer,	1033 7th street n. w.
*Rover, John W.	1861	Priest, S. J.	
Rover, Thomas A.	1860	Merchant,	741 N. Capitol street.
Rowland, John C.	1861	Phonographer,	607 6th street n. w.
Rowland, John Shannon	1864		
Ryan, William F.	1876	Clerk, Pension, Office,	811 I street n. w.
Sargent, Nathan			
Sands, George	1867	Lt. U. S. Navy,	
Sands, Joseph H.	1867	R. R. Director,	Roanoke, Va.
Sansbury, Thomas O.	1875		
Sardo, Joseph	1864	Advance Agent,	916 10th street n. w.
Saul, John A.	1875	Florist,	621 7th street n. w.
Saul, William J.	1874	Florist,	621 7th street n. w.
Scala, William F.	1869	Druggist,	
Schaffer, Ambrose L.	1876		

NAME.	YEAR.	OCCUPATION.	RESIDENCE.
Schaffer, Augustus L.	1880		
Schaefer, Charles 'i.	1867		
Schaffer, William E.	1875	Druggist,	517 E street n. w.
Schuerman, Charles	1865	Commission, Smithson.,	916 D street n. w.
Schuerman, Thomas	1967		
*Semmes, Alexander H.	1876		
Semmes, James H.	1860	Merchant,	740 12th street n. w.
*Senseney, George E.	1868		
Senseney, Francis T.	1868	Clerk,	615 G street s. w.
Sheckells, James	1869	Merchant,	1262 16th street n. w.
Sheckells, John H.	——		
*Sheckells, John W.	1865		
Shaw, Lemuel J.	1882		
Shaw, William B.	1882		
Shiel, Thomas W.	1864	Printer,	1236 N. Jersey av. n. w.
Simms, Thomas F.	1865		
*Simms, Alexander P.	1870		
Smith, Joseph H.	1865		
Smith, George	1864		
Smith, William R.	1865		
Snow, Tristan Burgess	1867		
Spalding, William L.	1864	Clerk, Census Office,	945 K street n. w.
Starbuck, William	1861		21 O street n. w.
Stegmeier, George W.	1871		1324 L street n. w.
Stellwagen, Edward J.	1867	Real Estate,	Chicago, Ill.
Stephens, Thomas A.	1868	Architect,	709 12th street n. w.
Stephens, Walter E. J.	1880		
Stewart, Edward S.	1864		
Stewart, Eugene	1864		
Stewart, William J.	1867	Clerk,	10 7th street n. e.
Stugis, James G.	1869		
Sullivan, George N., A. B.	1868		
Sullivan, John C.	1874	Printer,	237 Mass. av. n. e.
Sullivan, John J.	1868		
Sullivan, William F.	1882		
Sullivan, W. Joseph	1881		
Sweeney, William H.	1862	Printer,	71 H street n. w.
Talburtt, George W.	1868	Clerk, War Department.	
Thomas, William	1863		
Thyson, William F.	1868		
Tobriner, Leon, A. M.,	1874	Lawyer,	606 I street n. w.
Torney, George H.	1863		
Trader, George	1865	Journalist,	1014 25th street n. w.
Trettler, Robert B.	1868	Stenographer,	629 O street n. w.
Turner, William E.	1878		
Tucker, Edward D.	1865	Builder,	326 4½ street n. w.
Tynan, Joseph D.	1871	Merchant,	Corner 16th and L streets.
Tynan, William J.	1871	Student, S. J.,	Woodstock College.
Upperman, William B.	1868	Telegrapher,	513 11th street n. w.
Usher, John	1865		Indiana.
Usher, Linton J.	1866		Indiana.
Usher, Samuel C.	1866		Indiana.
Vatier, Charles A.	1877		
Voight, Edward B.	1874	Jeweler,	724 6th street n. w.
Wade, Louis	1865		
Wall, Howard C.	1865	Book-keeper,	412 6th street n. w.
*Walsh, Albert M.	1864		
*Walsh, Joseph	1863		
Walsh, James Francis	1863	Druggist,	300 L street s. e.
*Walsh, John A.	1871		
Walsh, Joseph W.	1861	Druggist,	1448 Corcoran av. n. w.
Walsh, Louis C.	1869	Clerk, Census Office,	1448 Corcoran av. n. w.
Walsh Redmond D.	1874	Lawyer,	St. Louis, Mo.
Walsh, Walter E.	1873		
Walsh, William	1873	Journalist,	
Walter, Charles A.	1875	Lawyer,	419 3d street n. w.
Ward, Francis M.	1872	Clerk, Patent Office,	527 6th street n. w.
Ward, James A.	1869	Lawyer,	
Waters, Robert W.	1865	Collector,	227 D street n. w.

58   GONZAGA COLLEGE.

NAME.	YEAR.	OCCUPATION.	RESIDENCE.
Wells, Isaiah	1868		
Wheatley, Joseph M.	1869	Merchant,	131 F street n. w.
White, John	1868	Merchant,	815 N street n. w.
White, William A.	1871		
Whiting, Francis	1867	Teller,	1917 G street n. w.
Whiting, Richard H.	1867		
Wilcox, Samuel M.	1881	Student,	503 A street s. e.
Willard, Edwin H.	1868		
Willard, Everett	1868		
Williams, Eugene J.	1867		
Williams, Francis D.	1863	Clerk,	9 Myrtle street n. e.
Williams, Thomas H.	1867		
Williams, William F.	1861	Clerk, Treasury,	906 14th street n. w.
Williamson, George A.	1863		
Wilson, Ignatius B.	1865		
Wilson, John C.	1861	Lawyer,	1006 F street n. w.
*Wilson, Matthew	1865		
Wilson, Samuel	1865		
Wilson, William	1865		
Wimsatt, Philip J.	1864		
Wimsatt, Samuel	1864	Merchant,	
Wimsatt, William A.	1871	Agent,	H near 9th street s. w.
Wolf, Samuel	1868		
Wood, Stanhope	1867		
Wordley, Willis H.	1860		
Woodward, Luther Thomas	1865	Printer,	515 Mass av. n. w.
Woodward, James S.	1872	Physician,	
Wright, Daniel W.	1868		
Watson, Francis	1863		
Young, John W.	1879	Clerk.	636 R. I. av. n. w.
Zappone, Claude R.	1870	Clerk, Signal Office,	Augusta, Ga.
Zell, Charles F.	1868	Builder,	319 13½ street n. w.
Zell, Enoch F.	1872	Builder,	615 7th street n. w.
Zell, George R.	1869		
Zell, Oliver	1871		
Zell, Raymond B.	1873		

Works Cited

Alexander, Frederick Warren, Ed. *Stratford Hall and the Lees Connected With Its History*. Oak Grove, VA: F. W. Alexander, 1912.

Arnold, Samuel Bland. *Memoirs of a Lincoln Conspirator*. Ed. Michael W. Kauffman. Westminster, MD: Heritage Books, 2003.

Balsiger, David and Sellier, Charles E., Jr. *The Lincoln Conspiracy*. Los Angeles: Schick Sunn Classic Books, 1977.

Barclay and Company. *Life and Extraordinary Adventures of John H. Surratt*. Philadelphia: Barclay & Co., 1867.

Bishop, Jim. *The Day Lincoln Was Shot*. NY: Harper & Row, 1955.

Blackman, Ann. *Wild Rose: Rose O'Neale Greenhow, Civil War Spy*. New York: Random House, 2006.

Brown, George Rothwell. *Washington: A Not Too Serious History*. Baltimore: The Norman Publishing Co., 1930.

Brownstein, Elizabeth Smith. *Lincoln's Other White House: The Untold Story of the Man and His Presidency*. Hoboken, NJ: John Wiley & Sons, Inc., 2005.

Bryan, Wilhelmus Bogart. *A History of the National Capital*, Vol. II. New York: The MacMillan Company, 1916.

Buckingham, J. E., Sr. *Reminiscences and Souvenirs of the Assassination of Abraham Lincoln*. Washington: Press of Rufus H. Darby, 1894.

Chamlee, Roy Z., Jr. *Lincoln's Assassins: A Complete Account of Their Capture, Trial, and Punishment*. Jefferson, NC: McFarland & Co., 1990.

Clark, Asia Booth. *John Wilkes Booth: A Sister's Memoir*. Ed. Terry Alford. Jackson, MS: University Press of Mississippi, 1996.

Commager, Henry Steele. *Illustrated History of the Civil War*. New York: Promontory Press, 1976.

Conley, Rory T., Ph.D. *The Truth in Charity: A History of the Archdiocese in Washington*. France: Èditions du Signe, 2000.

Cottrell, John. *Anatomy of an Assassination*. New York: Funk & Wagnalls, 1966.

Curran, Robert Emmet, S. J. "From Academy to University, 1789-1889." *The Bicentennial History of Georgetown University.* Vol. I. Washington, D.C.: Georgetown University Press, 1993.

Doster, William, *Lincoln and Episodes of the Civil War.* New York: G.P. Putnam's Sons, 1915

Durken, Joseph T. *William Matthews: Priest and Citizen.* New York: Benziger Brothers, 1963.

Furgurson, Ernest B. *Freedom Rising: Washington in the Civil War.* New York: Vintage Books, 2004.

Gonzaga College: An Historical Sketch. Washington, D.C.: National Capital Press, Inc., 1922.

Good, Timothy S. *We Saw Lincoln Shot: One Hundred Eyewitness Accounts.* Jackson, MS: University Press of Mississippi, 1995.

Goodrich, Thomas. *The Darkest Dawn: Lincoln, Booth, and the Great American Tragedy.* Bloomington, IN: Indiana University Press, 2006.

Goodwin, Doris Kearns. *Team of Rivals: The Political Genius of Abraham Lincoln.* New York: Simon & Schuster, 2005.

Hanchett, William. *The Lincoln Murder Conspiracies.* Urbana: University of Illinois Press, 1983.

Hayman, Leroy. *O Captain!: The Death of Abraham Lincoln.* New York: Four Winds Press, 1968.

Jones, Paul John, Ed. *Dr. Mudd and the Lincoln Assassination: The Case Reopened.* Conshohocken, PA: Combined Books, Inc., 1995.

Jones, Rebecca C. *The Mystery of Mary Surratt: The Plot to Kill President Lincoln.* Centreville, MD: Tidewater Publishers, 2004.

Kauffman, Michael W. *American Brutus: John Wilkes Booth and the Lincoln Conspiracies.* Westminster, MD: Heritage Books, 2005.

Kunhardt, Dorothy Meserve and Kunhardt, Philip B., Jr. *Twenty Days.* New York: Castle Books, 1965.

Laughlin, Clara E. *The Death of Lincoln: The Story of Booth's Plot, His Deed and the Penalty.* New York: Doubleday, Page & Co, 1909.

Leonard, Elizabeth D. *Lincoln's Avengers: Justice, Revenge, and Reunion After the Civil War.* New York: W. W. Norton & Company, Inc., 2004.

Lewis, Lloyd. *Myths After Lincoln.* New York: The Press of the Readers Club, 1941.

MacGregor, Morris J. *A Parish for the Federal City: St. Patrick's in Washington, 1794-1994.* Washington, D.C.: The Catholic University of America Press, 1994.

McCarty, Burke. *The Suppressed Truth About the Assassination of President Lincoln.* Haverhill, MA: Arya Varta Publishing Company, 1924.

McGreevy, John T. *Catholicism and American Freedom: A History.* New York: W. W. Norton & Company, Inc., 2001.

Moore, Guy W. *The Case of Mrs. Surratt: Her Controversial Trial and Execution for Conspiracy in the Lincoln Assassination*. Norman, OK: University of Oklahoma Press, 1954.

Mudd, Nettie, Ed. *The Life of Dr. Samuel A. Mudd*. Bowie, MD: Heritage Books, 1990.

Murray, R. L. *The Redemption of the Harper's Ferry Cowards: The Story of the 111th and 126th New York Volunteers at Gettysburg*. 4th ed. Wolcott, New York: Benedum Books, 1994.

Oldroyd, Osborn H. *The Assassination of Abraham Lincoln*. Washington, D.C.: O. H. Oldroyd, 1901.

Pinsker, Matthew. *Lincoln's Sanctuary: Abraham Lincoln and the Soldiers' Home*. Oxford, NY: Oxford University Press, 2003.

Proctor, John Clagett, LLD. Proctor's Washington and Environs. *Washington Sunday Star*, 1949.

Roscoe, Theodore. *The Lincoln Assassination, April 14, 1865*. NY: Franklin Watts, Inc., 1971.

Shelton, Vaughan. *Mask for Treason: The Lincoln Murder Trial*. Harrisburg, PA: Stackpole Books, 1965.

Steers, Edward, Jr., *Blood on the Moon: The Assassination of Abraham Lincoln*. Lexington, KY: The University Press of Kentucky, 2001.

_____, Ed. *The Escape and Capture of John Wilkes Booth*. Gettysburg: Thomas Publications, 1983.

_____, *Still Mudd: The Case Against Doctor Samuel Alexander Mudd*. Gettysburg, PA: Thomas Publications, 1997.

_____, Ed. *The Trial: The Assassination of President Lincoln and the Trial of the Conspirators*. Lexington, KY: The University Press of Kentucky, 2003.

Sullivan, Eleanore C. *Georgetown Visitation: Since 1799*. Washington, D.C.: Georgetown Visitation Monastery, 2004.

Swanson, James L. *Manhunt: The Twelve-Day Chase for Lincoln's Killer*. New York: HarperCollins Publishers, 2006.

Swanson, James L. and Weinberg, Daniel R. *Lincoln's Assassins: Their Trial and Execution*. Arena Editions, 2001.

Tayloe, Benjamin Ogle. *Our Neighbours on La Fayette Square: Anecdotes and Reminiscences*. Washington, D.C.: The Junior League of Washington, 1982.

Tidwell, William A. *Come Retribution: The Confederate Secret Service and the Assassination of Lincoln*. Jackson, MS: University Press of Mississippi, 1988.

Townsend, George Alfred. *Katy of Catoctin or the Chain-Breakers: A National Romance*. Cambridge, MD: Tidewater Publishers, 1959.

_____. *The Life, Crime, and Capture of John Wilkes Booth*. Kila, MT: Kessinger Publishing, 2004.

Trindal, Elizabeth Steger. *Mary Surratt: An American Tragedy*. Gretna, LA: Pelican Publishing Company, Inc., 1996.

Turner, Thomas Reed. *Beware the People Weeping: Public Opinion and the Assassination of Abraham Lincoln*. Baton Rouge, LA: Louisiana State University Press, 1982.

Vidal, Gore. *Lincoln: A Novel*. New York: Ballantine Books, 1985.

Warren, Paul and Dolan, Michael, Eds. *Echo Ever Proudly: Gonzaga College High School in the Press 1821-1899*. Washington, D.C.: Gonzaga Alumni Governing Board, 2005.

Wearmouth, Roberta J. and Wearmouth, John M. *Thomas A. Jones: Chief Agent of the Confederate Secret Service in Maryland*. Port Tobacco, MD: Stones Throw Publishing, 1995.

Weichmann, Louis J. *A True History of the Assassination of Abraham Lincoln and of the Conspiracy of 1865*. Floyd E. Risvold. Ed. New York: Random House, 1977.

Winik, Jay. *April 1865: The Month That Saved America*. New York: HarperCollins Publishers, 2001.

About the Author

Paul Warren is publisher of Warren Communications News in Washington, D.C., which publishes *Communications Daily* and *Consumer Electronics Daily,* among other news publications. He is co-editor of *Echo Ever Proudly*: *Gonzaga College High School in the Press 1821-1899* and a 1968 graduate of Gonzaga. He holds a bachelor's degree from Le Moyne College, Syracuse, N.Y., and was a reporter for the *Rochester* (N.Y.) *Times-Union* and the *Hornell* (N.Y.) *Evening Tribune*. In addition, he has written for the *New York Daily News*, the *Sporting News* and *TV Guide*.

His ancestor, Hiram Moses, a Union physician in the 111th N.Y. Volunteers, was one of thousands of Union troops captured by Confederates in a battle at Harper's Ferry in 1863. Also captured then was Boston Corbett, who was credited with shooting John Wilkes Booth. Among the Rebels capturing these Union soldiers was Lewis Powell, who would hang for his attempt to kill Secretary Seward and for plotting to kill Lincoln. Another blood relative of Warren's, Mary Ann Peper, married a distant cousin of Mary Todd Lincoln, Union Col. Luzerne Todd.

10488210R00086

Made in the USA
Charleston, SC
08 December 2011